jill dupleix's
fast food

jill dupleix's
fast food

photography by geoff lung

conran OCTOPUS

Commissioning Editor Suzannah Gough
Consultant Cookery Editor Jenni Muir
Editor Helen Woodhall
Editorial Assistant Maxine McCaghy

Art Editor Sue Storey
Food Stylist Jill Dupleix
Props Stylist Sibella Court
Photographs Geoff Lung
Production Suzanne Sharpless

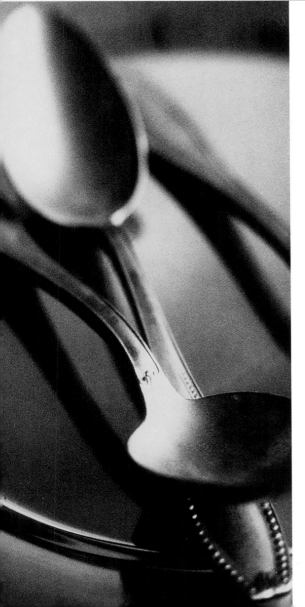

contents

introduction

Take three, and make yourself a meal ... prawns, chilli, ginger; pork, apple, sage; sardines, rocket, red pepper; ricotta, honey, pine nuts.

Food is a language best kept simple, so let's keep it short, sweet and straight to the table. Let's put flavour and freshness before fuss and bother.

Let's make every ingredient count, by shopping well, by cooking fast, and by eating slow. Let's think about colour, texture and flavour, and let them contrast, collide and collaborate.

Each recipe in this book is built on three major players, with a small supporting cast to be found in any well-stocked pantry.

When you cook with very few ingredients, each one has to be a star, so get rid of that ugly crowd of extras hanging around, and go for less food, more impact. Because the natural simplicity of food is the most civilized thing the world has to offer. Simple food is never boring. Simple food has balance and beauty. It is food at its best, in its natural shape and form. Taking something pure and raw and turning it into something exotic and unrecognizable is not what this is about. Besides, it takes too long.

Food that is bland and mass-produced is food that needs a lot more work and refinement to make it interesting. Why bother? Instead, start with the natural, fresh and unrefined produce.

Good food sets you free: like pasta, tomato, basil; chicken, ginger, soy; coffee, chocolate, rum. Take three, and remind yourself how simple life can be.

food is a language
best kept simple

The main thing to remember is that your three ingredients must be best friends: able to sleep together and still talk to each other in the morning. They don't have to be similar to be compatible, as anyone who has embarked on a long-term relationship (more than three days) will know.

Go for big flavours at the height of their ripeness.

Seek out punchy contrasts – steak with blue cheese; lemon with chicken; prosciutto with pears; lamb with pesto.

Reduce and intensify flavours: oven-roast tomatoes, onions, beetroots, peppers and aubergines for an hour in a moderate oven until their water content significantly reduces and flavours intensify.

Combine flavours with a highly developed sense of menage à trois. Find that illicit third partner to make the original couple exciting. Chicken and rocket are yawn material until lemons come along. Figs and honey are okay, but they soar when hit with tangy yogurt. Tuna and radicchio are desperate for crisp bacon.

Char-grill aubergines, courgettes, and red peppers. Marinate them in olive oil and herbs and use them in a hundred different ways.

Reduce the flavours of stocks, sauces, broths and juices by simmering, allowing the liquid to evaporate and intensify.

Roast the unroastable, and discover a wonderful new world of flavour: asparagus, corn cobs, carrots, courgettes, risotto, ricotta cheese, whatever. Particularly whatever.

Poach fruits, and use the cooking juices as a syrupy sauce. Reduce fruit juices into sticky syrups with a little sugar and spice.

Incorporate reduced flavours into butters and mayonnaise for instant flavour additives. Try Parmesan butter on pasta, avocado butter on prawns, saffron butter on fish.

Double up. If using lemon juice, grate the rind as well, and add a wedge to the plate. If there's bacon in there, crisp an extra rasher and crumble on top. Don't throw out the leaves of baby beetroots: cook them and serve under the beetroots. It's called resource management, and it's a smart thing to do.

staples

You've got breakfast cereal, right? Then at least you won't starve. But we're talking about feeding yourself and others without getting embarassed. We're talking about having enough good things on hand to turn out a great meal in minutes.

We're not talking about starting your own food hall; just about stocking up on the odd can of bamboo shoots and water chestnuts for instant stir-fries. Keeping a store of anchovies, capers, olives, sun-dried tomatoes and artichoke hearts for spontaneous weekend lunches. Feeding off a big wedge of Parmesan cheese in the fridge and having pasta, noodles and a few cans of tomatoes and tuna in the cupboard.

If you have onions and garlic, you can cook anything. Chillies are terrific. And, always, always, lemons, just in case you get a wild and crazy urge for a piece of grilled fish or a decent gin and tonic.

Feel free to use quality convenience foods like five-minute polenta, canned beans and somebody else's home-made pickles, with no added guilt. At least you're cooking.

You don't need all the stuff on this list. Build your pantry slowly, season by season. Stretch out the big investment items with more affordable everyday stuff. And always buy one thing you've never tried before in your life.

good
cooking
starts with
good
shopping

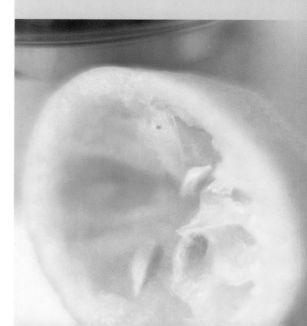

fresh

Buy these things regularly, or you will probably die.

Milk Fresh

Bread Great, long-lasting, naturally leavened sourdough.

Butter Salted or unsalted, it's up to you.

Eggs Free range, because it's nicer to the hens.

Lemons Heavy and juicy. Warm them slightly before squeezing them to get extra juice.

Onions White, brown, red, whatever you like.

Garlic Smash each clove with your fist, peel off the skin, and cook. Fish it out later, if you remember.

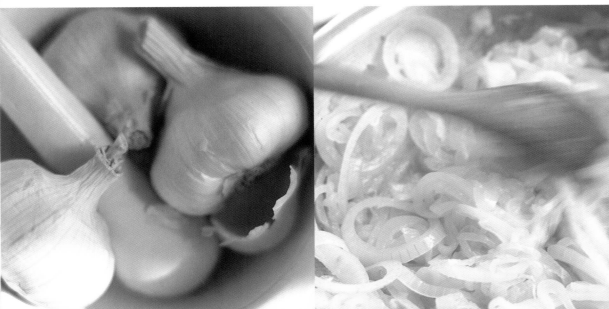

pantry

Anchovy fillets in oil

Apricots, dried

Bamboo shoots, canned. Drain and rinse. If they smell very bambooey, drop into boiling water for 2 minutes before using.

Bamboo skewers

Bay leaves

Beans, white, canned

Black beans, salted. Fermented, salted black beans, available in cans or packets from Asian food stores. Rinse well before using.

Black peppercorns

Breadcrumbs, dried

Capers, small and salted

Chicken stock in the freezer

Chillies, dried – long, dried red chillies are a Malaysian staple. Hang them in your kitchen and they'll last forever. Either grind to a powder, or soak in hot water for an hour, then whizz in the food processor with a little of the water and add the purée to your cooking.

Chilli oil Available in small bottles of highly concentrated hot stuff from Asian food stores.

Chinese rice wine known as *shao hsing*, this is the 'cooking brandy' of China, used to add complexity and flavour by the spoonful. It costs very little and is available at Asian food stores. Or substitute with dry sherry. I don't recommmend drinking it.

Chinese shiitake mushrooms, dried. Buy the neatest and largest type available, for the best flavour. Soak them in hot water for at least 30 minutes, then drain and cut off and discard the stem before using. You can use the soaking water to add flavour to your cooking, but strain it first to get rid of any grit.

Chocolate, dark (bitter) cooking (couverture)

Coffee beans

Cognac, or your favourite liqueur

Cornflour (cornstarch)

Crisp-fried shallots Small deep-fried shallots available by the jar in oriental food stores. Saves an awful lot of work.

Five-spice powder A pre-mixed spice blend available from supermarkets and oriental food stores, usually made up of star anise, cinnamon, cloves, fennel and Sichuan peppercorns.

Flour, plain

Herbs, especially mint and oregano

Honey

...music
to cook by

Instant dashi powder Made of ground dried bonito (fish) and konbu (kelp), this is a wonderfully easy way of making the mother-stock of Japanese cooking. Available from Japanese food stores and health food stores. Mix 10g (1/3 oz) of instant dashi powder with 500ml (18fl oz) hot water.

Mayonnaise, superior brand

Mirin Sweet Japanese rice wine, available from oriental food stores.

Music, to cook by

Mustard, Dijon

Oils Extra-virgin olive oil, vegetable or peanut oil, sesame oil

Oyster sauce Dark, thick, oyster-flavoured sauce thickened with cornflour (cornstarch), available from oriental food stores.

vodka in the freezer for drinking

Parmesan cheese, preferably in a wedge

Pasta, dried. Your favourites.

Pernod

Pickled onions

Rice, Arborio, jasmine, basmati

Rice wine vinegar A mild, sweet vinegar made from fermented rice. Substitute with a good white wine vinegar.

Saffron threads

Sake A clear wine brewed from rice used in Japanese cooking. Cooking sake is available from oriental food stores.

Salmon canned in oil, superior brand.

Sansho chilli pepper, Japanese. The ground, dried red pod of the prickly ash, used to add heat to many Japanese dishes.

Sea salt

Sesame oil A rich, powerful oil made of hulled, toasted sesame seeds. Use sparingly in Chinese cooking.

Soy sauce A fermented soy-bean product, available in both light (thin and salty) or dark (aged, less salty). If in doubt, use Japanese soy.

Spices, caraway seeds, ground cumin, ground coriander, cinnamon sticks, whole nutmeg, paprika

Sugar, brown, white, caster, icing

Sweet chilli sauce A thick, sweet, seedy chilli sauce used in Thai cooking.

Tea leaves, green

Thai fish sauce A thin, dark, pungent, and quite salty sauce made from fermented fish (*nuoc mam* in Vietnam, *nam pla* in Thailand, *patis* in the Philippines).

Tomato passata (puréed and sieved tomatoes)

Tomato purée (paste)

Tomato sauce or tomato ketchup

Tomatoes, canned

Tuna, canned in oil, superior brand

Vanilla pods (beans)

Vinegar, balsamic, red wine, white wine

Vodka, in the freezer, for drinking.

Water chestnuts The crisp round corms of a type of watergrass, available fresh or canned.

Wine, red and white, for drinking and cooking

Salt is sea salt.

Pepper is freshly ground black pepper.

Olive oil is extra-virgin for salads and drizzling, light for frying. Use peanut or vegetable oil for oriental dishes.

Sugar is normal old white table sugar or soft brown sugar.

An **egg** is 50–60g (2–2½ oz).

1 tbsp **butter** is 15g (½ oz)

A knob of **fresh ginger** is around 2.5cm (1in).

Tomatoes and **corn** are canned or fresh.

To **simmer** is to cook at a gentle bubble, not a rolling boil.

Follow either **metric** and **imperial** measurements. (It's like **male** and **female** – follow one or the other, not both, or you'll get into trouble.)

The day you leave your cereal box behind is the day you really grow up. And the day you leap out of bed and whisk gracefully into the kitchen to create a minor masterpiece without the slightest mess is the day you will never live to see. The thing is, it's morning. Sadly, breakfast comes at a time when you are at your most vulnerable. (Read: mascara smudges, bad hair, can't find kitchen.) You've just woken up. You're not up to speed yet. So go easy on yourself. Stack avocado and bacon on thick toast. Dollop yogurt on fruit crumble. Feast on a ripe mango. Still not awake? Then have your breakfast for lunch instead. But don't let anyone else cook you breakfast without thorough research into their habits, religion, background and sexual preferences. Breakfast is personal. Besides, they don't know where the coffee is, or how you like your toast. (Nor do you sometimes, but that's another matter.) Likewise, don't ever cook breakfast in bed for anyone else. It's far too presumptuous.

breakfast

corn

basil

tomato

crunchy corn fritters, frizzled tomatoes and fresh basil make a meal to look forward to all night

main players:

2 corn cobs, or 450g (1lb) canned corn kernels,

    drained

1 large bunch basil

450g (1lb) ripe tomatoes

staples:

2 tbsp extra-virgin olive oil

150ml (5fl oz) milk

150g (5oz) plain flour, sifted

2 eggs

1/2 tsp paprika

1 tsp baking powder

1 tsp sugar

sea salt and freshly ground black pepper

Peel the husks from the corn cobs and use a sharp knife to shear the kernels from each cob. Wash the basil and shake dry. Pick off about 20 leaves, and slice them into fine shreds. Slice the tomatoes thickly.

Heat half the oil in a non-stick frying pan and fry the tomatoes over a medium heat on both sides until lightly golden and soft. Set aside in a warm place.

Combine the shredded basil, milk, flour, eggs, paprika, baking powder, sugar, salt and pepper in a large bowl and stir well to make a smooth thick batter.

Put corn kernels in a bowl and add enough batter to just cover them – keep it ridiculously corn kernelly – and toss to coat.

Heat the remaining oil in a non-stick frying pan until hot, and drop 4 large spoonfuls of the mixture into the pan. Fry until golden, turning once. Keep the corn fritters warm while making four more.

Stack the corn fritters with tomato on each warmed serving plate and serve with extra sprigs of basil. **Serves four**

a golden omelette folded over smoky grilled asparagus and melting goat's cheese

main players:

450g (1lb) thin asparagus, trimmed

150g (5oz) fresh goat's cheese

12 eggs

staples:

2 tbsp extra-virgin olive oil

25g (1oz) butter

sea salt and freshly ground black pepper

eggs

asparagus

cheese

Brush the asparagus with olive oil and scatter with salt and pepper. Grill it, or cook it on a ridged cast-iron griddle, for 5–10 minutes, turning once, until tender.

Slice the cheese into eight slices. Set aside.

For each omelette, break 3 eggs into a bowl, season with salt and pepper and beat lightly with a fork. Heat a quarter of the butter in a non-stick frying pan. Pour in the eggs and cook over a medium heat. As the edges set, draw them back with a fork and allow the egg to run underneath and cook.

When the omelette is very nearly set, place two slices of cheese on one half of the surface and top with a layer of warm asparagus. Tip the pan slightly and fold over the top of the omelette with a fork, then slide it onto a warm plate and serve. Clean the pan, add a little more butter, and repeat for the remaining omelettes.

Makes four omelettes

avocado

bacon

toast

a fast stack of creamy avocado, crisp bacon and warm tomatoes on garlicky grilled bread

main players:

8 thin rashers bacon

4 thick slices sourdough bread

1 avocado

staples:

400g (14oz) can whole plum (roma)
*   tomatoes*

1 garlic clove, peeled and cut in half

1 tbsp olive oil

sea salt and freshly ground black pepper

Arrange the bacon on a foil-covered baking tray and grill until crisp – or fry in a non-stick frying pan. Drain on kitchen paper.

Gently remove the whole tomatoes from the can, without breaking them, and heat over a low heat in a saucepan until warm.

Grill the bread on both sides, then rub one side with the cut clove of garlic and paint it with a little olive oil.

Meanwhile, cut the avocado in half and remove the stone. Peel off the skin and cut each half into thick slices.

Place the grilled bread on serving plates and top with the bacon and avocado. Scatter with salt and pepper, and top with tomatoes and more bacon. Serve hot.

Serves four

peaches

summer fruit topped with a crunchy muesli crumble, served up warm in the morning

figs

muesli

main players:

6 ripe peaches

6 ripe figs

100g (3¹/₂ oz) muesli

staples:

1 tbsp caster sugar for fruit, plus

  2 tbsp for crumble

85g (3oz) butter

100g (3¹/₂ oz) plain flour

Heat oven to 200°C/400°F/Gas 6. Wash and dry the peaches and figs. Cut the peaches into bite-size chunks, discarding stones, but do not peel. Cut the figs lengthwise into quarters. Arrange in a rough tumble in a shallow buttered pie dish or baking tray. Scatter sugar over the top.

Cut the butter into tiny pieces and combine with the flour in a bowl. Rub the flour and butter together with your fingertips until clumpy. Mix with the muesli and sugar. Sprinkle with a little water and mix it through with a fork, leaving it quite lumpy.

Scatter the crumble topping on top of the fruit, and bake for around 40 minutes, until the fruit is bubbling hot and the topping is lightly golden.

Serve hot, warm or cold. **Serves four**

top rich buttery, toast with **smoked salmon** and a scramble of egg for a lazy Sunday breakfast of **simple luxury**

eggs

salmon

brioche

main players:

1 loaf brioche or sourdough bread

10 eggs

8 slices smoked salmon

staples:

2 tbsp milk

25g (1oz) butter, plus extra for spreading

sea salt and freshly ground black pepper

Cut four thick slices of bread and set aside. Heat the grill.

Break the eggs into a bowl, and add the milk, and salt and pepper. Gently break up the eggs with a fork.

Melt the butter in a non-stick frying pan, and scramble the eggs over a fairly low heat, stirring and scraping constantly with a wooden spoon, until they are cooked but still moist and bouncy. Meanwhile, toast or grill the bread, being careful not to burn it.

Butter the toast and arrange on serving plates. Top with soft folds of smoked salmon, and great spoonfuls of scrambled egg. Serve immediately. **Serves four**

panettone

plums

yogurt

grilled Italian **fruit bread** served with a sweet compote of plums and **plenty** of Greek yogurt

main players:

450g (1lb) blood plums

1 panettone, or other fruit bread

300ml (10fl oz) Greek yogurt

staples:

250g (9oz) caster sugar

1 cinnamon stick

1 vanilla pod (bean), split

Combine the sugar, cinnamon stick and vanilla pod with 500 ml (18fl oz) of cold water in a small pan and heat, stirring, until the sugar has fully dissolved. Add the plums, and poach gently for 10–15 minutes until tender. Their skins will slide off happily as they cook. Allow the plums to cool in the syrup, then remove them, and strain the syrup to remove the skins. Return the plums to the strained syrup. If you are superorganized, do this the night before.

Cut the panettone horizontally into four round slices, about 2cm (1in) thick, and set them aside.

Heat the grill, and grill the panettone on both sides, watching carefully, because it burns very easily. See? It burnt in the time it took to read that last sentence.

Arrange freshly grilled, unburnt panettone on serving plates, and top with poached plums and their syrup. Top with yogurt and serve. **Serves four**

the Sunday roast: a perfectly **poached egg** on top of sizzled bacon and **soft, sweet** roasted pumpkin

main players:

500g (1lb 2oz) pumpkin

8 thin slices prosciutto, bacon or pancetta

4 eggs

staples:

2 tbsp extra-virgin olive oil

2 tbsp white wine vinegar

sea salt and freshly ground black pepper

Heat oven to 200°C/400°F/Gas 6. Hack the pumpkin into four chunky wedges (peel it if you like, but you don't have to) and arrange on a baking tray. Scatter with salt and pepper and drizzle with olive oil. Bake for an hour until the wedges are soft and golden brown.

Arrange the prosciutto or bacon slices flat on a sheet of foil, then bake or grill for a few minutes until crisp.

To poach the eggs, fill a wide shallow pan with water to a depth of 5cm (2in) and bring to a rolling boil. Add the vinegar, which will help the whites to set. Turn off the heat, crack open an egg and drop it quickly but carefully into the water. Repeat with the remaining eggs.

Cover the pan immediately, and check after 3 minutes. The whites should be set, but the yolk should still be soft and runny.

pumpkin

Remove with a slotted spoon and drain on several folds of kitchen paper. Trim any messy edges with scissors.

Arrange the pumpkin on four serving plates, tuck in the prosciutto or bacon slices, and top with a poached egg.

Serves four

prosciutto

egg

rice

prunes

figs

a bowl of **creamy risotto** studded with fat, juicy prunes and figs leaves packaged cereal for dead

main players:

300g (10oz) Arborio rice

200g (7oz) pitted prunes

200g (7oz) dried figs

staples:

1 litre (1³/4 pints) milk

1 vanilla pod (bean), split

175g (6oz) soft brown sugar

Heat the milk and vanilla pod to simmering point. Add the rice and cook for 2–3 minutes, stirring, then reduce heat to very low – and I mean very low, or the whole thing will boil up and over – and cover. Cook gently for 15 minutes until the rice is tender and almost all of the milk has been absorbed, stirring occasionally.

In the meantime, combine 250ml (9fl oz) water with the sugar in a small pan and bring to the boil, stirring. Add the prunes and figs, and simmer for 20 minutes, stirring occasionally, until they are plump, sweet and tender.

Serve a ladleful of sweet risotto in each bowl, and spoon the warm fruits and their cooking juices on top. **Serves four**

sweetened ricotta and baked rhubarb are linked by warm berries melting into a sauce

main players:

450g (1lb) rhubarb, trimmed and washed

450g (1lb) fresh ricotta cheese

1 punnet raspberries or other berries

staples:

3 tbsp soft brown sugar

1 tbsp white sugar

Heat oven to 180°C/350°F/Gas 4. Cut the rhubarb stalks in half.

Place ricotta cheese in a small baking dish, and cover with foil. Arrange a layer of rhubarb on the base of another small baking dish and scatter with brown sugar and 2 tablespoons of water. Bake both the ricotta and rhubarb for 30 minutes.

Remove the foil from the ricotta, scatter with white sugar and bake for another 10 minutes, uncovered, until lightly golden. In the meantime, scatter the rhubarb with berries and bake for another 10 minutes until the berries and rhubarb are soft, and a syrup has formed.

Cut the ricotta into wedges and divide among serving plates. Top with rhubarb and berries, and a spoonful of cooking juices. **Serves four**

ricotta   rhubarb   berries

soft, warm Mexican quesadillas filled with a gentle melt of fresh mozzarella cheese and wilted spinach

tortilla

cheese

spinach

main players:

2 large bunches spinach, washed

1 mozzarella cheese or 6 bocconcini (small mozzarella balls)

8 flour tortillas, 18cm (7in) diameter

staples:

sea salt and freshly ground black pepper

Roughly chop the spinach, discarding stalks. Stuff it into a large saucepan with 250ml (9fl oz) of water and jam on the lid. Bring to the boil and cook gently for 5 minutes until it wilts to a glossy green mass. Remove, drain and cool. When cool, squeeze the spinach in your hands to wring out excess water. Chop finely and set aside.

Slice the cheese finely and set aside. Heat a non-stick frying pan for 1 minute over a moderate heat. Lay out 4 tortillas and spread each one with a quarter of the spinach, right to the edges. Arrange slices of cheese over the top and scatter with salt and pepper. Top with another tortilla.

Place one tortilla sandwich in the hot pan and dry-fry for 2–3 minutes until the cheese just starts to soften. Turn carefully and fry on the other side. Slide out of the pan onto a plate and keep warm while you make the remaining sandwiches. Cut each one into six wedges and serve. **Serves four**

The best thing about making your own

lunch is that you know where it's been. Why pay good money for a lousy focaccia stacked with oily cushions of unrecognizable drabness in a café full of nonentities, when you can stay home for lunch and eat something absolutely gorgeous in the company of stylish, fabulous people such as yourself? Lunch needs a sense of the silly to be successful. Reinvent the ploughman's lunch, the school lunchbox, the office sandwich and the street-stall snacks of Asia. Then mix them all up and forget I said anything. Nobody said lunch had to be sensible. Besides, it's the middle of the day and time to relax. Not you, silly. Your food. It needs to take it easy for a while, take a break from dressing up and working too hard. Food gets stressed too, you know.

lunch

prawns

tomato

halloumi

a **new** look at a Greek classic; the acid **freshness** of tomato **shakes** up sweet prawns and salty cheese

main players:

32 small raw prawns or 24 medium prawns

6 ripe plum (roma) tomatoes

200g (7oz) halloumi cheese

staples:

3 tbsp extra-virgin olive oil

2 lemons

freshly ground black pepper

Heat oven to 180°C/350°F/Gas 4. Devein the prawns by inserting a fine bamboo skewer through the back and hooking out any black intestinal tract. Peel them, leaving the tails on. Thread three or four prawns onto eight skewers and set aside.

Cut the tomatoes in half lengthwise. Arrange them, cut side up, on a baking tray, brush with a little of the olive oil, and bake for 30 minutes until soft and lightly browned. Juice one of the lemons and cut the other into quarters.

Cut halloumi into four 1cm (½ in) thin sheets. Heat a little of the olive oil in a heavy pan and fry the cheese on one side only until golden. Turn out the cooked cheese onto serving plates.

Brush the prawns with olive oil and fry them quickly, turning just once, in a non-stick pan over a high heat until the flesh turns opaque.

Arrange 2 or 3 oven-roasted tomato halves on top of each slice of cheese, and lean two skewers of prawns against the stack. Drizzle with olive oil and lemon juice, and scatter with black pepper. Serve with lemon wedges. **Serves four**

a sizzle and a stir – when the tomatoes **just burst** at their seams, your **lunch is ready**

main players:

450g (1lb) cleaned squid tubes

250g (9oz) cherry tomatoes

1 small bunch basil

staples:

4 anchovy fillets

2 tbsp olive oil

freshly ground black pepper

squid

tomato

basil

Clean and rinse the squid tubes, then slice into rings about ½in (1cm) wide. Drain the anchovy fillets. Wash the tomatoes and shake dry. Pick the leaves off the basil and discard the stems.

Gently warm the olive oil in a frying pan and fry the anchovies until they start to melt. Turn up the heat and add the squid tubes, tossing well for 1–2 minutes until the flesh turns opaque.

Add the tomatoes and toss well, allowing most of the tomatoes to soften and explode, bursting their juices through the sauce. Add most of the basil leaves and the pepper and stir through quickly. Serve piled high on serving plates scattered with the remaining basil leaves. Try this on its own, with a green salad, as a pasta sauce, or over soft polenta. **Serves four**

beef

pickles

cheese

a glamorous play on the ploughperson's lunch – rare roast beef, Cheddar cheese and pickled onions

main players:

400g (14oz) beef fillet

200g (7oz) Cheddar cheese

4 pickled onions

staples:

3 tbsp extra-virgin olive oil

1 tbsp white wine vinegar

1 tsp Dijon mustard

sea salt and freshly ground black pepper

Grill the beef on all sides for around 10 minutes until well-marked on the outside but still rare inside.

Remove from the heat and allow to rest for 30 minutes. Slice the cheese and onions into very thin slices.

To serve, slice the rested beef into 1cm (1/2 in) thick slices, and season with salt and pepper. Layer the beef and cheese on each plate and top with sliced onions. Fish out any pickling spices from the jar of onions and use them as well.

Whisk the olive oil, vinegar, mustard, salt and pepper in a bowl, and drizzle over the top. (Or beat the mustard into a good quality mayonnaise and serve on the side.)
Serves four

artichokes

earth meets sea in this rustic stick of artichoke hearts and fresh tuna, scented with bay leaves and drizzled with olive oil

tuna

lemon

main players:

2 x 300g (10oz) thick tuna steaks

12 artichoke hearts in olive oil

1 lemon

staples:

12 bay leaves

sea salt and freshly ground black pepper

Trim the tuna steaks of all blood lines and cut into 24 small cubes, each measuring about 2.5cm (1in). Sprinkle with salt and pepper. If the artichoke hearts are on the large side, cut them in half. Reserve the oil they are in.

Thread tuna and artichoke hearts onto eight bamboo skewers, separating them occasionally with the bay leaves. (Make sure you pierce the tuna against the grain, so that it doesn't flake off the skewer.) Cut the lemon into eight wedges and attach a wedge to the end of each skewer.

Brush the tuna, artichoke hearts and lemon wedges with some of the oil from the artichoke hearts, or extra olive oil. Heat a large non-stick frying pan, and fry the tuna sticks for 2 minutes on either side, until the fish is slightly crusty, but still pink inside.

Brush the extra lemon wedges with oil and quickly fry. Serve tuna sticks with fried lemon wedges and drizzle with a little extra olive oil. **Serves four**

sizzling prawns with a cool-as-a-cucumber Greek yogurt dressing

main players:

1 cucumber

450ml (16fl oz) Greek yogurt

12 medium raw prawns

staples:

1 tsp salt

2 garlic cloves, peeled and crushed

1 tbsp white wine vinegar

1 tbsp olive oil, plus extra for frying

cucumber

yogurt

prawns

Peel, deseed and finely chop the cucumber. Sprinkle it with the salt and leave to drain for an hour or so. In the meantime, place the yogurt in a wrap of two sheets of cheesecloth or muslin and hang to drain over a bowl.

After 1 hour, squeeze out any excess water and place the yogurt in a bowl. Beat in the garlic, vinegar and olive oil. Squeeze any excess water from the cucumber and stir into the yogurt.

Devein the prawns by inserting a fine bamboo skewer through the back and hooking out any black intestinal tract. Peel the prawns, leaving the tails on. Brush with a little olive oil and grill or pan-fry quickly until cooked.

To serve, stack prawns on four serving plates and spoon cucumber and yogurt sauce on top. **Serves four**

fish

tomato

chilli

a **tangy Thai dish** you can do in the time it takes to **cook the rice**

main players:

350g (12oz) canned plum (roma) tomatoes

1 tbsp sweet chilli sauce

4 fresh snapper or red bream fillets, skinned

staples:

2 tbsp vegetable oil

2 onions, finely chopped

2 tbsp lime juice

sea salt and freshly ground black pepper

steamed jasmine rice to serve

Heat the oil in a frying pan and cook the onions for 10 minutes over a moderate heat until soft but still pale. Chop the tomatoes finely, saving all the juices, and add them to the pan with the sweet chilli sauce, salt and pepper. Add 250ml (9fl oz) water, cover and cook for 10–15 minutes until the sauce thickens.

When the sauce is ready, slide the fish fillets into the simmering sauce and cook for a few minutes only, until the flesh turns opaque and flakes easily.

Add lime juice to the sauce, and taste for a final balance of chilli, lime, salt and pepper. Serve with plenty of steamed jasmine rice.

Serves four

clams

beans

mint

a warm Italian salad of fresh baby clams, spiked with mint and served with cannellini beans: the perfect summer lunch

main players:

900g (2lb) baby clams (vongole)

450g (1lb) canned white beans

1 small bunch mint

staples:

4 tbsp extra-virgin olive oil, plus extra

for drizzling

115ml (4fl oz) white wine

freshly ground black pepper

Clams can be salty, so soak them in cold water for 30 minutes, then drain, replace water and soak for another 30 minutes. Drain the canned beans and rinse well. Pick the leaves from the mint stalks.

Heat half the olive oil, the white wine and half the mint leaves in a heavy frying pan with a lid. When bubbling, add the drained clams and cover tightly. Cook over a high heat for 2 minutes, then remove the lid. Using tongs, remove all the clams that have opened, then give the pan a big shake, and just keep removing the clams as they open. Place the cooked clams in a bowl and cover to keep warm. Throw away any that don't open, as they're not fresh.

When you have picked out all the clams, drain the pan juices through a piece of dampened muslin or a fine sieve into a small bowl. Gently warm the remaining olive oil in a frying pan, and add the drained beans, remaining mint and pepper. Add a spoonful or two of the pan juices.

When the beans are heated through, add the clams, toss through once or twice, and divide among four bowls or serve on a large serving platter. Serve warm or at room temperature. Drizzle with oil before serving. **Serves four**

sake

salmon

radish

Japanese minimalist art, **perfectly** steamed salmon with a pinch of grated radish sits in a pool of sweet sake broth

main players:

4 x 200g (7oz) salmon fillets

1 long white radish (daikon)

200ml (7fl oz) sake

staples:

10g (1/3oz) instant dashi powder

2 tbsp soy sauce

2 tbsp mirin

1 tbsp sugar

sea salt

Skin salmon and use tweezers to remove any fine bones. Cut a cross into the flesh of each fillet and scatter lightly with salt.

Peel the white radish and grate until you have enough to fill 2 tablespoons. Set aside in a sieve to drain. Cut the remaining radish lengthwise into very thin long strips.

Bring plenty of water to the boil in a steamer. Arrange strips of radish on a heatproof plate and place the salmon fillets on top. Pour sake over the salmon, cover with foil and steam for 8–10 minutes until the salmon is just cooked through and flakes easily.

To make the broth, combine instant dashi powder with 250ml (9fl oz) water and bring to the boil. Add the soy, mirin and sugar and heat, stirring, until the sugar has completely dissolved.

Divide the long strips of radish and salmon between four small Japanese bowls, then pour the broth around each salmon piece.

Squeeze out any excess moisture from the grated radish and arrange a big pinch of it on top of each salmon fillet. Serve with spoons and chopsticks. **Serves four**

sardine

rocket

red pepper

the **crisp** texture and oily flesh of the sardine plays off sweet red pepper and **peppery** rocket leaves

main players:

4 red peppers (capsicums)

12 fresh sardines, filleted

200g (7oz) baby rocket leaves

staples:

4 tbsp extra-virgin olive oil

125g (4^1/$_2$oz) dry breadcrumbs

1 tbsp red wine vinegar

1 tbsp tiny capers, rinsed

sea salt and freshly ground black pepper

Heat oven to 180°C/350°F/Gas 4. Rub a little of the olive oil over the skin of the peppers and roast on a baking tray for 30 minutes until scorched and blistered. Remove from the oven and place in a covered bowl for 10 minutes. Peel off the skins, cut in half and discard seeds but save the juices. Cut the flesh into wide strips and set aside.

Clean and dry the sardines, then brush lightly with a little of the olive oil. Press each side into the breadcrumbs. Heat the remaining olive oil in a frying pan and quickly fry the sardines until lightly golden on both sides.

Wash and dry the rocket leaves. Whisk the vinegar and 3 tablespoons of the pepper juices with the capers, salt and pepper, and toss the rocket lightly in the dressing.

Divide the rocket leaves between four serving plates. Top with folds of roasted red pepper, and arrange the sardine fillets on top. Spoon over any remaining dressing and serve. **Serves four**

shells of pasta filled with a **quick stir** of warm tomatoes and **fresh** basil – **summer** on a plate

pasta

tomato

basil

main players:

6 large ripe tomatoes

1 small bunch basil

20 large pasta shells (conchiglie or lumache)

staples:

2 tbsp extra-virgin olive oil, plus extra for pasta

2 tsp sugar

sea salt and freshly ground black pepper

Dunk the tomatoes in a pan of boiling water for 30 seconds, then peel off the skins, cut in half, squeeze to remove seeds, and chop the remaining flesh.

Heat the olive oil, tomatoes, half the basil leaves, sugar, salt and pepper and cook for around 15 minutes over a medium heat until the tomatoes are soft and sweet, and almost soupy.

Cook the pasta shells in plenty of salted, boiling water until tender, but still firm to the bite.

Drain the pasta and toss the shells in a little olive oil to prevent them sticking. Gently toss pasta shells in the tomato and basil sauce, making sure the sauce slips inside the shells. Add the remaining basil leaves and toss quickly. Divide between four pasta bowls and serve. **Serves four**

crisp-fried prawns and fish in a beer batter, served with deep-fried lemon slices

main players:

400ml (14fl oz) flat beer

4 x 150g (5oz) fresh white fish fillets,
  such as cod or hake

8 medium raw prawns

staples:

175g (6oz) plain flour

1 tsp soft brown sugar

2 lemons

vegetable oil for deep-frying

sea salt and freshly ground black pepper

To make the batter, mix the flour, sugar, salt and pepper in a large bowl. Add the beer slowly, whisking until smooth and thick. Set aside for 10 minutes.

Trim the fish into portions the size of a large forefinger. Devein the prawns by inserting a fine bamboo skewer through the back and hooking out any black intestinal tract. Peel them, leaving the tails on.

Slice one lemon as finely as possible, and dry each slice with kitchen paper. Cut the other lemon into quarters.

Heat the oil until it starts to smoke. Dip the pieces of fish in batter until well coated and deep-fry until golden. Remove and drain on kitchen paper. Do the same with the prawns, and then the lemon slices.

Arrange the fish and prawns in piles on four serving plates, and top with deep-fried lemon slices and lemon wedges. Serve with a cold glass of beer, of course. **Serves four**

fish

prawns

beer

chicken wings marinated in Japanese flavours and grilled until golden

main players:

10 chicken wings

2 tbsp grated fresh ginger

3 spring (green) onions, finely chopped

staples:

3 tbsp sake

3 tbsp soy sauce

3 tbsp mirin

1 lemon, quartered

sea salt

steamed rice to serve

Wash the chicken wings and wipe dry. Cut off the wing tips. Bend each wing until you can see the joint, then cut through with a sharp knife. Rub each piece with salt.

Mix the grated ginger and most of the spring onions with the sake, soy and mirin. Toss the chicken wings in the marinade until well coated, cover with plastic film and leave for at least 30 minutes.

Heat the grill or a cast-iron griddle. Drain the wings, reserving the marinade, and cook on both sides until half cooked, for around 10 minutes. Coat in the marinade once more, then cook for a further 10 minutes, or until golden and tender (chicken always takes longer to cook than you think), turning once or twice. Scatter with the remaining spring onions and serve with lemon wedges and steamed rice. **Serves four**

chicken

onions

ginger

Don't let the kitchen get in your way. It's not a relentlessly tidy shrine; a space dedicated solely to the processing of food. It's just a place where violence meets entertainment and comes up with something to eat. Keep it fuelled up and ready to service you when you need it. Walk in, fix yourself a drink, open the fridge, start up the stove, and chop an onion. If you can chop an onion, you can cook dinner any time, anywhere, for anyone. If you also own a sharp knife, a fat chopping board, a good pan and a grill that works, then that's about as good as it gets.

The only other thing you need is the food itself. Buy the best, and you'll eat better as well as faster. If you start with great stuff, you need to do very little to make it better. The best thing about staying at home to cook, of course, is that you eat so well. That, and the fact that you don't have to think about putting on enough clothes to appear decently in public.

dinner

beef

courgette

red pepper

grilled beef fillet with Mediterranean vegetables, topped with a dollop of garlicky aïoli

main players:

400g (14oz) beef fillet, tied with string

2 medium-sized courgettes (zucchini)

2 red peppers (capsicums)

staples:

2 garlic cloves, peeled

½ tsp sea salt

2 egg yolks

300ml (10fl oz) good, fruity olive oil,
*   plus extra for peppers*

2 tbsp lemon juice

freshly ground black pepper

To make the aïoli, crush the garlic and salt together until mushy. Beat in the egg yolks until you have a creamy paste. Add the olive oil really slowly – drip by drip at first, then a little faster – beating constantly, until you have a thickened sauce. Beat in the lemon juice and pepper to taste. Lighten the aïoli if need be, by beating in a little warm water. (You can do all this in the food processor or by hand.) Refrigerate until needed.

Grill the beef on all sides until well-marked but still rare inside, around 8 minutes. Remove it from the heat and allow to rest for 10 minutes.

Cut the courgettes lengthwise into thin strips, and cut each pepper lengthwise into four quarters, discarding the core and seeds. Brush with a little olive oil and grill or fry in a ridged cast-iron griddle on both sides until blistered and soft.

To serve, cut off the string and slice the beef into 1cm (½in) thick slices. Pile the courgettes and red pepper in the centre of each plate and top with sliced beef. Add a spoonful of aïoli on top and serve.

Serves four

a **sweet** and mushy baked apple becomes a **juicy sauce** for a **simply** cooked pork chop

main players:

4 Granny Smith apples

8 sage leaves, chopped

4 thick pork loin chops

staples:

250ml (9fl oz) white wine

1 tbsp of butter

1 tbsp extra-virgin olive oil

sea salt and freshly ground black pepper

Dijon mustard to serve

Heat oven to 180°C/350°F/Gas 4. Core the apples and score the skins to stop them splitting. Place them in a baking tray, add the white wine and bake for 45 minutes until the apples are soft and squishy.

Heat the butter, oil and sage leaves in a frying pan. Add the pork chops and cook over a moderate heat for 8–10 minutes.

Season with salt and pepper. Turn once, scooping up the cooked sage leaves and place them on top of each chop. Cook the remaining side for 5 minutes until tender.

In the meantime, gently remove the apples from their cooking juices, pour the juices into a pan and boil furiously until the liquid is reduced to around 125ml (4fl oz).

Place a pork chop on each plate, top with a baked apple and spoon over the juices. Serve with Dijon mustard. **Serves four**

pork

sage

apple

fresh salmon meets creamy avocado and the citrus tang of grapefruit

avocado

grapefruit

salmon

main players:

2 large ripe avocadoes

2 ripe grapefruit, peeled

4 x 150g (5oz) fresh salmon fillets, with skin

staples:

2 tbsp lemon juice

4 tbsp extra-virgin olive oil, plus 1 tbsp extra for frying

sea salt and freshly ground black pepper

Whisk the lemon juice, olive oil, salt and pepper in a large bowl to make a dressing.

Cut an avocado in half lengthwise. Hit the stone with the blade of a large knife, then turn the knife to twist out the stone. Peel off the skin and cut the flesh into chunks, dropping them directly into the dressing. Repeat with the remaining avocado.

Trim any white pith from the grapefruit. Cut into small segments and add to the dressing along with any extra juices. Toss lightly, and chill for 10 minutes or so.

Heat the remaining oil in a heavy pan and cook the salmon, skin-side down, until the skin is crisp and the flesh turns pale pink. Turn and cook on the other side, leaving the salmon soft and pink in the middle.

Place the salmon, skin side up, on serving plates and top with a big spoonful of avocado and grapefruit. Spoon the juices around the salmon and serve. **Serves four**

chicken

prosciutto

peas

tender chicken breast **wrapped** in prosciutto and roasted, served on a bed of **squishy peas**

main players:

4 x 150g (5oz) chicken breast with skin and

   wing attached

8 thin slices prosciutto

600g (1lb 5oz) fresh or frozen peas

staples:

2 tbsp extra-virgin olive oil

500ml (18fl oz) chicken stock or water

1 tbsp butter

sea salt and freshly ground black pepper

Heat oven to 180°C/350°F/Gas 4. Heat the oil in a frying pan until hot. Add the chicken portions, skin-side down, and sear each breast until lightly browned on both sides, for about 5 minutes. Remove and drain on kitchen paper.

Wrap each chicken portion in two slices of prosciutto, securing it with a wooden cocktail stick if need be. Transfer to an ovenproof dish, add a few spoonfuls of stock or water to the pan, and bake for 10–12 minutes. Remove and allow to rest for 5 minutes before serving.

Cook the peas in the remaining chicken stock or in simmering, salted water for 10 minutes until tender (5 minutes for frozen peas), then remove from the heat and drain into a heatproof bowl, reserving the liquid.

Add the butter to the peas, and roughly mash with a potato masher. Add the cooking liquid back into the peas, spoonful by spoonful, beating with a wooden spoon. Stop when the peas have absorbed enough liquid to be moist and squishy. Serve a big dollop of peas in the centre of each plate and top with chicken. **Serves four**

red pepper

chick peas

cous cous

golden grains of fruity cous cous served with grilled vegetables and a spicy tomato sauce

main players:

4 red peppers (capsicums)

2 x 400g (14 oz) cans chick peas

450g (1lb) cous cous

staples:

8 dried apricots

2 tbsp extra-virgin olive oil

400g (14 oz) can plum (roma) tomatoes

1/2 tsp ground cumin

1 tbsp butter

sea salt and freshly ground black pepper

Soak the apricots in 250ml (9fl oz) of warm water for 30 minutes. Cut each red pepper lengthwise into 3 sections and remove the inner core. Brush with the olive oil and grill on both sides until well marked.

Whizz half the grilled red peppers in a food processor with the tomatoes and their juices, cumin, salt and pepper. Transfer to a saucepan. Drain the chick peas and rinse well under cold running water. Drain again, add to the sauce, and simmer gently for 10 minutes.

Drain the apricots and cut into slices. Combine with the cous cous in a heatproof bowl. Add the butter and 400ml (14fl oz) boiling water and stir through. Cover and keep warm for 5 minutes while the cous cous expands, then fluff it up with a fork.

Turn out the cous cous onto a large warmed serving plate and arrange the grilled pepper slices on top. Pour the red pepper sauce over the top and serve at the table so that everyone can help themselves.

Serves four

a **cold night** calls for desperate measures and a hearty rice dish that needs
a good **bottle of red** as much as you do

main players:

3 Italian pork sausages

300g (10oz) Arborio rice

115ml (4fl oz) good red wine

staples:

1 tbsp butter

1 onion, finely chopped

750ml (1¼ pints) hot chicken stock

1 tbsp grated Parmesan cheese, plus

extra for sprinkling

sea salt and freshly ground black pepper

Heat a non-stick frying pan. Skin the sausages and pinch small sections of them into the pan. Fry gently until lightly crusty and golden, then completely drain off any fat, and set aside the sausage meat in a warm place.

Melt the butter in a heavy saucepan, add the onion and cook over a moderate heat until it softens. Add the rice and toss until well coated in butter, stirring constantly. Add the red wine and allow it to bubble and be absorbed for 2 minutes, stirring. Add the sausage and stir through.

Add the chicken stock and bring back to the boil. Reduce the heat to very low, cover and cook for 15–20 minutes until the rice has absorbed the stock and is tender.

Add the Parmesan, stir, taste for salt and pepper, and serve with extra grated Parmesan. **Serves four**

rice   red wine   sausage

sweet, scorched lamb chops with the flavour of a Cantonese roast meats stall, served with crisp Chinese broccoli

main players:

8 or 12 well-trimmed ('Frenched')

   lamb chops

3 tbsp hoi sin sauce

1 Chinese broccoli (gai laan)

staples:

2 tbsp soy sauce

2 tbsp sugar

1 tbsp rice wine or dry sherry

1/2 tsp five-spice powder

1/2 tsp salt

1 tsp sesame oil

For well-trimmed chops, it is best to buy whole racks of lamb and ask the butcher to cut through the bones, or simply chop through the final linked bone with a Chinese cleaver.

Combine hoi sin, soy sauce, sugar, rice wine, five-spice powder and salt in a large bowl and add the lamb chops. Leave to marinate for 1 hour, turning once or twice.

Heat the grill or barbecue. Drain the chops and grill, turning once or twice. The outer meat will scorch as the sugars caramelize – which is good – but be wary of burning, and remove the chops while the lamb is still pink and tender inside.

Meanwhile, chop the broccoli into 5cm (2 in) sections, dividing the stems from the leaves. Cook the stems in simmering, salted water for 2 minutes, then add the leaves and cook for up to 1 minute until they soften. Remove and drain in a colander.

Arrange a neat layer of stems on four warmed serving plates, and top with leaves. Drizzle the greens with sesame oil, lean 2 or 3 lamb chops against them and serve.

Serves four

lamb

hoi sin

greens

only **meaty, fresh** tuna can stand up to the slight bitterness of radicchio, the salt factor of bacon and the **sweet tang** of balsamic vinegar

main players:

4 x 250g (9oz) tuna steaks

2 heads radicchio

8 thin slices bacon or pancetta

staples:

1 tbsp extra-virgin olive oil, plus 2 tbsp
*   extra to serve*

2 tbsp balsamic vinegar, plus 2 tbsp extra
*   to serve*

Brush the tuna lightly with olive oil and grill or pan-fry on one side for 4 minutes, and on the other side for 2–3 minutes until the outside becomes slightly crusty but the inside is still rare.

Cut off the radicchio roots, separate the leaves and wash and dry them. If the leaves are very large, tear them in half lengthwise. Cut the bacon slices in half.

Heat a large non-stick frying pan and cook the bacon until crisp on both sides. Add the radicchio and toss over a high heat. Add the balsamic vinegar and keep tossing until the radicchio starts to soften and wilt.

Divide the wilted radicchio and most of the bacon between four warmed dinner plates. Place the grilled tuna steaks on top, and arrange a little bacon on top of the tuna. Drizzle with any cooking juices from the pan, and the extra olive oil and balsamic vinegar and serve. **Serves four**

tuna

radicchio

bacon

a fast 'choucroute' of cabbage **spiked** with caraway seeds lies beneath **gently poached** salmon

main players:

4 x 200g (7oz) fillets fresh salmon

½ medium white cabbage, around 1kg

(2lb 4oz), cored and finely shredded

10 small potatoes

staples:

sea salt

1 tbsp butter

200ml (7fl oz) white wine

1 tbsp white wine vinegar

2 tsp caraway seeds

Remove any skin and bones from the salmon and set aside.

Cook the potatoes (peeled or unpeeled, it's your call) in simmering, salted water for 15 minutes until tender.

Cook the cabbage in simmering, salted water for 10 minutes until still fairly crunchy, then drain well.

Melt the butter in a frying pan, add the wine and bring to the boil. Add the drained cabbage and toss well. Arrange the salmon fillets on top, cover tightly, and cook over a gentle heat for around 10 minutes until the cabbage is tender and the salmon is cooked but still pink and moist in the centre.

Gently remove the salmon fillets and keep warm. Add the vinegar and half the caraway seeds to the cabbage and toss well for 1 minute. Arrange a heap of cabbage on four warmed serving plates and top each with a salmon fillet.

Drain the potatoes, cut in half and tuck them around the salmon. Sprinkle with the remaining caraway seeds and serve.
Serves four

salmon

cabbage

potato

prawns

chilli

ginger

messy, juicy and downright delicious Singaporean chilli prawns in a lush, spicy tomato sauce

main players:

12 large raw prawns

5cm (2in) piece of ginger, peeled

2 tbsp sweet chilli sauce

staples:

2 tbsp vegetable oil

4 tbsp tomato sauce or ketchup

1 tbsp soy sauce

250ml (9fl oz) hot chicken stock

1/2 tsp sea salt

2 tsp sugar

1 heaped tsp cornflour, blended with
    1 tbsp cold water

Devein prawns by inserting a wooden bamboo skewer through their backs and hooking out the thin, black vein. Do not peel. Slice the ginger finely and cut each slice into thin matchsticks.

Heat the oil in a wok or frying pan and fry the ginger for 30 seconds over a high heat. Add the prawns and cook for a minute or two. Remove the prawns and ginger and set aside.

To the remaining oil in the wok, add the chilli sauce, tomato sauce, soy sauce, chicken stock, salt and sugar, and stir well to mix. Add the cornflour paste, bring to the boil and stir for 1 minute until the sauce thickens.

Return the cooked prawns and ginger to the wok and toss well for a couple of minutes to heat through until well coated in the sauce. Serve with plenty of noodles, or jasmine rice for mopping up the juices.

Serves four

veal

cheese

tomato

a last-minute melt of **fresh** cheese and tomato
with **crisply crumbed** tender veal

main players:

4 large or 8 small veal cutlets, on the bone

1 mozzarella or 6 bocconcini (small

   mozzarella balls)

4 small ripe tomatoes

staples:

3 tbsp plain flour

2 eggs

125g (4¹/₂oz) dry breadcrumbs

1 tbsp olive oil

1 tbsp butter

sea salt and freshly ground black pepper

Place each veal cutlet on a sheet of plastic film and cover with another sheet of plastic film. Use a meat mallet, or some other heavy murder weapon, to flatten the meat to a uniform 1cm (¹/₂in).

Sift the flour into a bowl and season well with salt and pepper. Beat the eggs in a shallow bowl. Place the breadcrumbs in a third bowl.

Slice the mozzarella and tomatoes and arrange in slightly overlapping layers on a foil-covered baking tray. Scatter with salt and pepper.

Heat the grill, and have four plates ready.

Heat the oil and butter in a heavy-bottomed frying pan. Dip each veal cutlet first in the flour, then the egg, then the breadcrumbs, and fry on both sides over a moderate heat until golden. Place the cheese and tomatoes under the grill (or in a hot oven) for a few minutes until the cheese starts to melt.

Drain the cutlets on kitchen paper, and arrange on each plate with the tomatoes and cheese. **Serves four**

dried **pasta** from Italy **comes to life** with green peas and that other **old faithful** – canned tuna

main players:

450g (1lb) dried tortellini

200g (7oz) fresh or frozen peas

200g (7oz) canned tuna in olive oil

staples:

sea salt and freshly ground black pepper

Cook the tortellini in a large pot of simmering, salted water, according to the packet instructions, then drain. Cook the peas in simmering, salted water until tender, and drain.

Combine the drained tortellini, peas, canned tuna with its olive oil, salt and pepper in a frying pan, and heat through, tossing gently.

Divide between four warmed pasta plates and serve. **Serves four**

tortellini

peas

tuna

You know you don't need it, but you want it. You deserve it. Damn it, you have a right to it. Just make it fresh, fruity, light and bright, and jump into it. Go beyond cream and ice-cream as additives, and think sweet syrups, a handful of toasted nuts and tangy yogurt instead. That way, you can have three helpings. Cream is just a habit you get into, like adding salt. It can mask the flavours until they die of creaminess. Chocolate, on the other hand, is a fine and wonderful thing that comes somewhere very soon after global peace on the list of things the world cannot do without. The trick is to go for sweet things that contribute more than just sugar to our lives. Toffeed figs. A mousse with the bittersweetness of espresso coffee. Fresh cheese drizzled with honey. Biscotti dipped into liqueur. Little sweetmeats to serve with mint tea. These are desserts that don't just sit there smiling sweetly, they do something.

dessert

are these **cute** or what? **little fruity** eclairs you build yourself from **sponge** fingers, ice-cream and a punnet of berries

main players:

400g (14oz) berry ice-cream

8 thin sponge finger biscuits

1 punnet strawberries, raspberries or blueberries

Take the ice-cream from the freezer and leave to soften for 5 minutes. Arrange a sponge finger biscuit on each plate.

Wash the strawberries, if using, and pull out and discard the green stems. Cut them in half lengthwise. Select the best-looking of the other berries, but don't wash them or they'll get soggy.

Place two scoops of ice-cream on each bottom biscuit, and then tuck in 3 or 4 berries. Top with the remaining biscuits and push down gently. Scatter the remaining berries around each plate and serve immediately, with no mucking about.

Serves four

ice-cream   biscuits   berries

toffeed figs topped with tangy yogurt and toasted walnuts, done in seconds

main players:

2 tbsp walnut kernels

6 large ripe figs, washed and dried

200ml (7fl oz) Greek yogurt

staples:

1 tbsp soft brown sugar

Heat a dry frying pan and lightly toast the walnuts for 1–2 minutes. Remove from the pan and crush lightly.

Heat the grill until really hot. Cut the figs in half lengthwise and sprinkle with sugar.

Grill the figs for 2–3 minutes until the sugar has melted and glazed and the figs are warm. Arrange 3 fig halves on each serving plate. Top with a dollop of yogurt and a scattering of crushed walnuts.

Serves four

walnuts

figs

yogurt

coffee

a **rich espresso** mousse that combines the well-matched **flavours** of coffee, chocolate and rum

main players:

175g (6oz) dark (bitter) chocolate

2 tbsp strong black prepared coffee, plus 1

tbsp ground coffee extra for sprinkling

1 tsp rum or brandy

staples:

4 eggs

Chop the chocolate into small pieces. Mix the chocolate with the prepared coffee in a bowl over a pan of simmering water, stirring until melted and smooth. Remove from the heat and allow to cool a little.

Separate the eggs, keeping the yolks in a small bowl and the whites in a large one.

Beat one egg yolk at a time into the cooled chocolate mixture, until they have all been incorporated. Add the rum and stir well.

Beat the egg whites until they form soft white peaks which are not too stiff.

Stir a large spoonful of egg white into the chocolate mixture to lighten it, then tip all the chocolate mixture into the egg whites and fold gently until mixed.

Spoon into individual pots or coffeecups and chill for 1–2 hours until firm. To serve, sprinkle with a little ground coffee.

Serves six

rum

chocolate

light **creamy** ricotta, cut from the round, drizzled with honey and **crunchy** pine nuts

main players:

450g (1lb) fresh ricotta

4 tbsp wild honey

2 tbsp pine nuts

Toast the pine nuts in a dry frying pan until lightly golden.

Place the ricotta on a serving plate. Dip a spoon in a cup of hot water, shake dry, then dip it into the honey and drizzle honey over the ricotta.

Scatter the lot with toasted pine nuts, and serve with spoons. **Serves four**

If you feel the need to do something more complicated (yeah, right) bake the ricotta in the oven according to the method described on page 27. Serve it warm, drizzled with honey and pine nuts. Or make the drunken prunes on page 78 and pour them over the top.

ricotta

honey

pine nuts

a little glass of **sweet** mint tea, with dainty sweetmeats **on the side**

main players:

175g (6oz) shelled walnuts

150g (5oz) dates, stoned

1 small bunch fresh mint

staples:

1 tbsp Chinese green tea leaves

sugar to taste

icing sugar for dusting

Lightly toast the walnuts in a dry frying pan until they smell fragrant.

Place the dates and walnuts in the food processor and blend until they form a paste. If the paste is a little dry, add a teaspoonful of water, rosewater or liqueur. Press a teaspoonful of the mixture into the palm of your hand, roll into a ball and set down on a small tray. Continue until the mixture is finished, making 12 balls, and refrigerate until needed.

To make the mint tea, place the tea leaves in a pot and top with boiling water, then strain off the water. Add more boiling water, a handful of fresh mint leaves, and a teaspoon of sugar per person. Stir, then strain into small heatproof glasses (place a teaspoon in the glass as you pour to avoid cracking).

Arrange each glass on a serving plate with a few sprigs of mint. Dust the sweetmeats with icing sugar through a sieve and arrange three on each plate. **Serves four**

mint

walnuts

dates

crisp fried wonton wrappers layer **ripe** mango and **creamy** yogurt

main players:

12 small square wonton dumpling wrappers

2 ripe mangoes

250ml (9fl oz) Greek yogurt

staples:

vegetable oil for deep-frying

icing sugar for dusting

Heat the oil in a small frying pan and deep-fry the wonton wrappers until crisp and golden. Drain on a cooling rack and dust with icing sugar through a sieve.

Peel the mangoes and cut each one into thick slices, working around the central stone. Squeeze the juices from the mango flesh attached to the stones into the yogurt and stir well.

Place 1 wonton wafer on each plate and top with a slice of mango. Drizzle with some of the yogurt, top with another wafer, more mango and more yogurt, finishing with a final wafer. Dust a little icing sugar on top and serve immediately.

Serves four

wonton

mango

yogurt

watermelon

rosewater

petals

pretty pink granita, an icy slush made glamorous with floating rose petals

main players:

600g (1lb 5oz) watermelon flesh,

without rind or seeds (reserve a few

seeds for garnish)

1 tsp rosewater

pink rose petals for serving

staples:

100g (3¹/₂oz) caster sugar

Combine the sugar with 125ml (4¹/₂fl oz) water in a small pan and bring to the boil, stirring until the sugar has dissolved. Remove from the heat and leave to cool.

Purée the watermelon flesh in a blender to give 500ml (18fl oz) of liquid.

Combine the watermelon purée, rosewater and cooled sugar syrup, and pour the mixture into a plastic container and place in the freezer.

Leave for 30–60 minutes – depending on the strength of your freezer – until it starts to freeze around the edges. Remove and stir well, breaking up the ice crystals, scraping the hard bits from the side. Return to the freezer and repeat the process every 30 minutes, for three or four times. The mixture will become increasingly thick and almost gluey, with very fine crystals.

Rinse the rose petals to remove any trace of chemicals and gently pat dry. Divide the granita between four small glasses or glass dishes, scatter with rose petals and a few reserved watermelon seeds and serve.

Serves four

Rosewater is available from supermarkets and Middle Eastern stores.

grab a spoon and dig in to **plump and potent** drunken prunes, served on a mound of **must-have** mascarpone

coffee

prunes mascarpone

main players:

2 tbsp ground espresso coffee

450g (1lb) large dried prunes, stoned

450g (1lb) mascarpone cream cheese

staples:

200g (7oz) sugar

3 tbsp brandy or Cognac

Dissolve the coffee in 125ml (4½fl oz) of boiling water, then strain, discarding any coffee grounds.

Heat the coffee, sugar, brandy and 250ml (9fl oz) water in a saucepan, and boil for 1 minute. Reduce the heat, add the prunes and cook at a slight bubble for 20 minutes, stirring occasionally, until the prunes soften and plump up and the liquid reduces to a syrupy consistency. If the liquid isn't very syrupy, bring to the boil and allow to bubble and reduce for a minute or two, watching carefully.

Remove from the heat and set aside, leaving the prunes in the liquid until ready to serve.

Place a big dollop of mascarpone in the centre of each serving plate and arrange a few of the prunes on top. Drizzle with the syrup and serve. **Serves four**

very cheeky – a sort of kid's drink-turned-cocktail-turned-dessert served in martini glasses – but very refreshing

main players:

450g (1lb) sorbet, such as berry or lemon

1 punnet fresh berries, such as raspberries

250ml (9fl oz) champagne – drink the rest

Chill four martini glasses until cold.

Arrange one or two scoops of sorbet in each one, depending on the size of glass, and scatter the sorbet with berries.

Very slowly and carefully – or it will fizz up too much – pour the Champagne on top until the sorbet is almost submerged. Serve immediately. **Serves four**

sorbet

champagne   berries

oooh, sexy. The perfect pear-shaped pear, generously draped with rich, dark, chocolate

main players:

6 brown-skinned pears

100g (3 1/2oz) dark (bitter) chocolate

250ml (9fl oz) double cream

staples:

850ml (1 1/2 pints) sparkling wine or water

300g (10oz) caster sugar

25g (1oz) butter, diced

50g (2oz) soft brown sugar

Combine the sparkling wine or water and caster sugar in a saucepan and bring to the boil, stirring. Wash the pears, but do not peel them. Place them in the syrup and simmer gently for 20–30 minutes, until tender to the touch. Allow the pears to cool in the syrup.

Finely chop the chocolate.

Combine the cream, butter and brown sugar in a small pan and heat, stirring, until the sugar has dissolved and the sauce is smooth. Remove from the heat, add the chopped chocolate and stir well until completely smooth.

Drain the pears well and place one pear in the centre of a shallow soup plate. Spoon the hot chocolate sauce over the top until the whole pear, including the stem, is completely coated. Repeat for the other pears. Serve immediately. **Serves six**

pears

chocolate

cream

oven-roasted peaches – as warm as if taken straight **from the sunshine** – served with a **nutty** liqueur and crisp biscuits for dipping

main players:

4 large ripe but firm freestone peaches

400ml (14fl oz) Italian Nocello or

Frangelico liqueur

12 dry Italian biscotti, such as cantuccini or

amaretti

Heat the oven to 180°C/350°F/Gas 4. Carefully cut a small slit around the circumference of each peach and place on a baking tray. Add a spoonful or two of water to the pan and bake for 30 minutes – slightly less for smaller peaches – until they are soft to the touch.

Carefully remove, without bruising, and leave to cool for 10 minutes.

Your choice now is to either leave the peaches looking rustic with their skins on, or to peel them off, which reveals their rosy shoulders. Your call.

Drizzle a little of the liqueur over each peach. Serve one peach per person on a dinner plate, next to a small glass of the same liqueur, and a few biscotti for dipping. **Serves four**

peaches   liqueur   biscotti

forget tiramisu – the world has **moved on**, to fresh berries, cream cheese and **melting** sponge fingers

main players:

1 punnet strawberries

450g (1lb) mascarpone cream cheese

450g (1lb) sponge finger biscuits

staples:

2 eggs

3 tbsp sugar

2 tbsp brandy or Italian liqueur

115ml (4fl oz) milk

Wash the strawberries, remove the green stem and cut in half lengthwise. Separate the eggs. Using a wooden spoon, beat the mascarpone with the sugar, egg yolks, and half the brandy or liqueur. In a separate bowl, whisk the egg whites until stiff and peaky, then gently fold them into the cheese mixture.

Combine the remaining brandy or liqueur and milk in a saucer and dip each biscuit into the mixture. Use them to line the base of a small square cake tin measuring 20 x 20cm (8 x 8in), breaking up the biscuits to fill in the corners as necessary.

Cover the biscuits with half the cheese mixture, then top with a layer of strawberries. Arrange another layer of soaked biscuits on top, another layer of cheese and a final layer of strawberries.

Chill for 4 hours, then serve in big, generous, sloppy spoonfuls. **Serves four**

berries

mascarpone

biscuits

If you wouldn't eat it on a plate, don't turn it into a soup. Soup is just food you eat with a spoon, after all. Break the rules. Open the cupboard. Liberate soup from the food police and tailor each bowl to suit: thick, thin, hot, cold. Add a handful of golden breadcrumbs, crisped bacon, melting cheese on toast, black olives, sizzled mushrooms, a spoonful of pesto or chilli jam. Forget anything you may have heard about soup being a first course. Soup can definitely be the main event. You don't even need a freezer full of stock. Cook a few leeks and carrots in a little butter and add boiling water for instant soup. Or just add water to a couple of chicken pieces and cook until it smells like soup (because it is soup). You can live on soup, if you're clever enough. Or if you don't have any knives and forks.

soup

sweet
potato

bacon

onion

smooth and **luscious** with a deep, mellow flavour, this is perfect for a cold winter night and plenty of **hot toast**

main players:

750g (1lb 10oz) sweet potatoes

8 thin, rindless bacon rashers

2 onions, finely chopped

staples:

1 tbsp extra-virgin olive oil

2 bay leaves

1.2 litres (2 pints) chicken stock

1/2 tsp freshly grated nutmeg

sea salt and freshly ground black pepper

Heat the oven to 180°C/350°F/Gas 4. Cut the sweet potatoes in half lengthwise, rub with the olive oil and bake, cut side down, for 1 hour until tender. Allow to cool, then scoop the flesh out of the skins and discard the skins.

Arrange the bacon on a foil-covered baking tray and grill or fry in a non-stick frying pan until super crisp. Remove and drain on kitchen paper, then crumble into small pieces. Cook the onions in the bacon fat or in 1 tablespoon of olive oil over a moderate heat for 5 minutes until they start to soften.

Add the sweet potato flesh, bay leaves, chicken stock, nutmeg, salt and pepper and bring to the boil, stirring. Simmer for 15 minutes, stirring occasionally. If it's too lumpy for your taste, whip out the bay leaves and whizz the whole lot in the food processor, otherwise leave it alone. Serve in warmed soup bowls, topped with crumbled crisp bacon. **Serves four**

hearty, rustic and homely – these words give you clues that this dish will look pretty ordinary, but taste great

main players:

1/2 medium white cabbage

400g (14oz) canned white beans

4 good quality pork sausages

staples:

2 onions

1 tbsp butter

1 tbsp extra-virgin olive oil

sea salt and freshly ground black pepper

Dijon mustard to serve

Slice the onions finely. Discard the outer leaves of the cabbage and slice the rest of it finely. Melt the butter and oil in a large frying pan, add the onions and cook for 15 minutes over a low heat until golden. Add the cabbage and cook for 5 minutes.

Add 1.5 litres (2½ pints) of boiling water, salt and pepper, and cook over a low heat for 20 minutes, stirring occasionally. Add the beans and cook for another 10 minutes, then taste for salt and pepper.

Meanwhile, prick the sausages and grill until browned. Divide the soup among four shallow soup bowls, top each one with a grilled sausage and serve with a pot of Dijon mustard that can be added at the table. Or slice the sausages thickly and arrange them in a ring in the centre of each bowl, and pour the soup over the top.
Serves four

cabbage

sausage

white beans

the nicest and fastest way to eat mussels – cook them in cider or champagne, and serve with a touch of cream

main players:

1.5kg (3lb 5oz) mussels

250ml (9fl oz) dry cider or champagne

100ml (3¹/₂fl oz) single cream

staples:

1 tsp black peppercorns

Soak the mussels in a bucket of cold water for 3 hours, changing the water twice so they are not too salty. Drain and scrub well, tugging off the little beards. Discard any that are cracked or stay open when you tap them.

Bring the cider and peppercorns to the boil in a large pan with a lid. Add the mussels, cover tightly and quickly bring to the boil.

Give the pan a big shake after 1 minute, and use tongs to take out any mussels that have opened. Put these in a large bowl.

Return the lid for another minute and repeat the process until you have removed all the opened mussels. Throw out any that do not open.

Divide the mussels between four warmed soup plates. Strain the cooking broth through a muslin-lined sieve into a bowl then put it back in the pan.

Add the cream and heat through, stirring, until smooth and then pour the broth over the top. **Serves four**

mussels   cider   cream

red pepper

a smooth, **ruby red** purée with a fresh **zippy flavour** and a suggestion of **spice**

tomato

olives

main players:

6 red peppers (capsicums)

350g (12oz) canned plum (roma) tomatoes

20 tiny black olives, stoned, or 2 tbsp tapenade,
   plus 4 olives, to serve

staples:

1/2 tsp ground cumin

1/2 tsp cayenne pepper

1.5 litres (2 1/2 pints) chicken stock

1 tbsp extra-virgin olive oil

sea salt and freshly ground black pepper

Heat oven to 200°C/400°F/Gas 6. Roast the red peppers on a baking tray for around 30 minutes until scorched and blistered. Transfer to a covered bowl for 10 minutes until cool enough to handle, then peel off the skins, catching the seeds and juices in the bowl. Strain out the seeds and keep the juices.

Combine the skinned red peppers with the cooking juices, tomatoes, cumin, cayenne pepper, salt and pepper in the food processor and blend until fairly smooth without over-blending.

Combine the red pepper mixture with the chicken stock and heat to a high simmer. If using black olives, finely chop, mash or purée them and mix with the olive oil.

Taste the soup for salt, pepper and spices. Add a spoonful of olive purée or tapenade to each bowl and serve topped with a whole olive. **Serves four**

tomato

leek

fish

splash around in a Mediterranean rockpool
of rich tomatoey seafood

main players:

3 tomatoes

3 leeks

450g (1lb) fresh white fish fillets, such as
   cod, hake, John Dory or monkfish

staples:

1 tbsp butter

1 tbsp extra-virgin olive oil

2 tbsp tomato purée (paste)

1.5 litres (2^1/$_2$ pints) fish stock or water

1 large pinch saffron threads

sea salt and freshly ground black pepper

Cut the tomatoes in half and squeeze out the seeds, then cut the flesh into small cubes. Trim the leeks and slice the white part finely. Rinse in cold water and drain.

Melt the butter and oil in a frying pan over a medium heat, add the leeks and cook until they are soft and gooey, about 20 minutes. Add the tomatoes, tomato purée, fish stock, salt and pepper, and stir well. Grind the saffron threads with the back of a wooden spoon in a few drops of warm water. Add the saffron to the pan, stirring. Simmer for 10 minutes.

Cut the fish into bite-size chunks, removing any skin or bones. Slip the fish into the broth and simmer for 5 minutes, until just cooked. Taste for salt and pepper and adjust accordingly.

Use a slotted spoon to divide the leeks and fish among four soup bowls, then pour the broth on top. **Serves four**

gentle Chinese flavours in a bowl: sweetcorn plays with sweet crab in a velvety, comforting dish

corn

crab

onion

main players:

2 corn cobs

175g (6oz) fresh crab meat

2 spring (green) onions, finely sliced

staples:

1.5 litres (2 1/2 pints) chicken stock

1 tsp cornflour, blended with 1 tbsp cold water

1 egg

sea salt

Peel the husks from the corn cobs and cook the cobs in simmering salted water for 10 minutes until tender. Cool, then scrape off the kernels with a sharp knife.

Bring the chicken stock to the boil in a saucepan, then reduce to a simmer. Add the crab and sweetcorn kernels and cook for 2 minutes, stirring. Add salt to taste, then stir in the cornflour paste and bring back to the boil, stirring.

Beat the egg lightly and pour it in a steady stream through the tines of a fork into the soup, whisking lightly so it forms long strands. The soup should be creamy, with a velvety texture and sweet taste.

Pour the soup into warmed Chinese soup bowls and sprinkle with the sliced spring onions. **Serves four**

miso

prawn

mushroom

light but full of flavour, this versatile Japanese soup could be breakfast, lunch or on the side at the dinner table

main players:

3 tbsp red miso paste

12 small or 6 medium raw prawns

12 oyster (abalone) mushrooms

staples:

25g (1oz) instant dashi powder

2 tbsp mirin

2 tbsp light soy sauce

Combine the instant dashi with 1 litre (1¾ pints) water and heat until just below boiling point. Add the mirin and soy sauce, stirring.

Remove 4 tablespoons of the broth and let it cool for a minute or two. Whisk it into the miso paste, then pour the miso liquid very slowly back into the hot dashi broth, stirring constantly until well blended. Do not allow it to boil.

Devein the prawns by hooking out the small intestinal tract along the back of each with a fine bamboo skewer. Peel the prawns, leaving the tail intact. Wipe the mushrooms clean with a damp cloth, and cut in half lengthwise, if large.

Add the prawns to the broth and cook for 3–4 minutes until they turn opaque. Add the mushrooms and cook for a further minute.

Divide the broth, prawns and mushrooms between four Japanese soup bowls and serve with chopsticks and china spoons.

Serves four

You will find miso paste, a fermented paste made from soya beans, in larger supermarkets, or in the refrigerated section at Japanese food stores or health food stores.

lentils

potato

onion

it's down-home and **hungry** time, with a hearty bowl of lentils simmered with **spices** and potato

main players:

2 potatoes

2 onions

300g (10oz) small brown or green lentils

staples:

1 tbsp butter

1 tbsp vegetable oil

400g (14oz) can plum (roma) tomatoes,

*   chopped*

^{1}/$_2$ tsp ground cumin

^{1}/$_2$ tsp ground coriander

^{1}/$_2$ tsp cayenne pepper

sea salt and freshly ground black pepper

Peel and finely chop the potatoes and onions. Melt the butter and oil in a frying pan, add the onions and cook for 15 minutes until the onions are soft.

Add the potatoes, lentils and 2 litres (3^1/$_2$ pints) boiling water and bring back to the boil, skimming off any froth if necessary. Reduce the heat, add the tomatoes, cumin, coriander, cayenne, salt and pepper, and stir well.

Simmer, partly covered, for 1 hour until the potatoes are cooked and the lentils are tender, stirring occasionally.

Taste for spices and adjust accordingly. Spoon into four warmed soup bowls and serve. **Serves four**

a chilled summer purée that really acts as a kind of exquisitely refreshing cocktail

cucumber

yogurt

mint

main players:

2 cucumbers

450ml (16fl oz) Greek yogurt

1 small bunch mint

staples:

450ml (16fl oz) chicken stock

1 tsp paprika

sea salt and freshly ground black pepper

Peel the cucumber and cut in half lengthwise, discarding seeds. Reserve a small amount to use as a garnish. Place the cucumber in a food processor, add the yogurt and mint and whizz until creamy.

Add the chicken stock, paprika, salt and pepper and whizz again to mix together. Pour into a jug or bowl and refrigerate for several hours.

Serve the soup in small bowls or in cocktail glasses, and top with an ice cube or two and the reserved cucumber. **Serves four**

bread

tomato

garlic

a soup that's really a salad: **sourdough** bread, rich, ripe tomatoes and your **fruitiest** olive oil

main players:

350g (12oz) stale sourdough bread

450g (1lb) ripe tomatoes

2 garlic cloves, peeled

staples:

100ml (3^1/$_2$fl oz) extra-virgin olive oil, plus extra
 to serve

1.2 litres (2 pints) chicken stock

1 small bunch basil

sea salt and freshly ground black pepper

Remove crusts from the bread, slice thickly and cut into 2cm (3/4in) cubes. Chop the tomatoes roughly, and squash the garlic with the side of a knife until flattened.

Heat the olive oil and garlic in a heavy saucepan. When hot, add the tomatoes and cook, stirring, for 5 minutes.

Add the chicken stock gradually, stirring, and bring to the boil. When the mixture is bubbling, add the stale bread cubes, salt and pepper, and cook, stirring, for another 5 minutes. Toss in a handful of fresh basil leaves and stir them through.

Cover and simmer over a very low heat for 20–30 minutes. Stir every now and then, squashing some of the bread into the soup with a potato masher or the back of a wooden spoon.

Remove from the heat and leave to cool for a while. Serve just warm, drizzled with extra olive oil. **Serves four**

Three things you should never find in a salad: alfalfa, grated carrot, and banana. Three things you should always find in a salad: freshness, crispness, contrast. Salad isn't lettuce. It's just like a normal meal, only it's younger, smarter, dressier, and more exciting to eat. Great salads also come in bottles. You want fruity extra-virgin olive oil, and vinegar with attitude – balsamic, champagne, sherry, walnut, or rice wine. Salads can be hot, cold, exotic or everyday. Warm salads have time to mingle and get to know each other, and you have time to do what you want instead of rushing to the table. Salads can be made from take-away chicken, pasta, tuna, beef, sausage, roast veggies and anything in the bottom of the fridge as long as it is sparkling fresh. And as long as it isn't alfalfa, grated carrot or banana.

salad

chicken

cucumber

celery

a crisp and crunchy plateful
of chicken and vegetables

main players:

2 chicken breasts

1 large cucumber

3 celery stalks

staples:

8 dried Chinese mushrooms

sea salt

2 tbsp soy sauce

2 tbsp rice wine vinegar or white wine vinegar

1 tbsp sesame oil

Soak the dried Chinese mushrooms in a bowl of warm water for 30 minutes, then rinse well. Trim the stalks off, squeeze dry and slice finely.

Poach the chicken breasts in a pan of simmering, salted water for 20 minutes, until cooked through. Drain, remove the skin and slice finely.

Peel the cucumber and cut it in half lengthwise. Scoop out and discard the seeds and cut the flesh into long matchsticks, or peel into long strips with a vegetable peeler. Slice the celery very finely, on the diagonal.

Mix the soy sauce, vinegar and sesame oil in a bowl and lightly toss the chicken, mushrooms, cucumber and celery in the dressing. Serve in oriental bowls with chopsticks. **Serves four**

a combination of **tangy Thai** flavours that practically jumps off the plate with freshness

chicken

mint

lime

main players:

2 chicken breasts

1 small bunch mint

4 tbsp lime juice

staples:

1 tbsp vegetable oil

1 tsp white or palm sugar

2 tbsp Thai fish sauce (nam pla)

1/2 tsp chilli powder

Rub the chicken breasts with vegetable oil and grill or pan-fry for about 15 minutes, until tender. Allow to rest.

Pick the mint leaves from the stalks and finely chop half, leaving the rest whole.

Stir the lime juice and sugar with the fish sauce, until the sugar dissolves. Remove the skin from the chicken and slice the breast finely on the diagonal.

Toss the chicken, chopped mint and chilli powder in the dressing, pile onto a plate, scatter with the whole leaves and serve.

Serves four

fresh fish mixed with **ripe** tomatoes and piquant leaves screams **sunny** holidays by the Mediterranean

main players:

450g (1lb) fresh fish fillets, such as cod

   or hake

3 ripe tomatoes

200g (7oz) baby rocket leaves or other

   small green leaves

staples:

250ml (9fl oz) white wine

2 bay leaves

1 lemon

2 tbsp small black olives

1 tbsp tiny capers, rinsed

4 tbsp extra-virgin olive oil

sea salt and freshly ground black pepper

Combine the white wine and bay leaves with 500ml (18fl oz) water and bring to the boil. Reduce the heat to a light bubble and add the cod. Simmer for 5 minutes until just cooked, then remove and cool.

Flake the fish into bite-sized pieces using your fingers or a knife.

Cut the tomatoes in half and squeeze out and discard the seeds and juice. Cut the flesh into small dice.

Wash and dry the rocket leaves. Juice the lemon.

Combine the rocket, tomatoes, olives and capers in a large bowl. Mix the olive oil with 2 tablespoons of the lemon juice, salt and pepper, and toss the salad lightly in the dressing. Add the flaked fish, lightly toss, and divide between four serving plates.

Serves four

cod

tomato

rocket

crisp, thin fennel and torn leaves mix it with buttery shards of Parmesan to make every mouthful an explosion

main players:

2 heads fennel

1 head radicchio

1 large bunch baby rocket leaves

staples:

1 small wedge Parmesan cheese

1 lemon

4 tbsp extra-virgin olive oil

sea salt and freshly ground black pepper

Wash and trim the fennel, and slice very thinly. Remove the outer leaves of radicchio, and wash and slice the heart into very fine strips. Wash and dry the rocket leaves.

Place the fennel and the salad leaves in a large bowl. Use a vegetable peeler to peel off thin shards of Parmesan, letting them drop onto a sheet of paper.

Squeeze 2 tablespoons of juice from the lemon and whisk it with the olive oil, salt and pepper to make a dressing. Pour the dressing over the salad and toss well. To serve, pile high in the centre of each plate. Scatter the Parmesan curls over each salad. **Serves four**

rocket

fennel

radicchio

egg

bacon

greens

finely sliced omelette links crisp matchsticks of bacon with curly endive

main players:

3 large eggs

4 rashers good bacon

1 bunch curly (frisée) endive

staples:

1 tbsp vegetable oil

1 tbsp white wine vinegar

3 tbsp extra-virgin olive oil

sea salt and freshly ground black pepper

Beat the eggs together in a small bowl.

Cut the bacon into thick matchsticks and fry in a non-stick frying pan until crisp. Drain the bacon on kitchen paper and set aside in a warm place.

Separate the leaves of the curly endive, wash well and dry. Cut off any stems.

Heat the vegetable oil in a wok or frying pan, tipping the pan to oil the entire surface. Pour the eggs into the pan and roll the pan around to coat the maximum surface possible with egg.

Move the pan around over the heat while the egg is cooking, until it is firm and no liquid remains. Place a large plate on top, and tip the pan upside down so that the omelette falls onto the plate (with luck).

Sprinkle the omelette with salt and pepper, roll up tightly and cut across the roll into very thin strips with a sharp knife.

Whisk the vinegar, olive oil, salt and pepper in a large bowl. Add the endive and toss well. Add the bacon and omelette, toss well and serve. **Serves four**

waxy hot potatoes contrast with fruity black olives and flakes of fish

main players:

600g (1lb 5oz) waxy potatoes

600g (1lb 5oz) canned tuna in olive oil

20 small black olives

staples:

4 tbsp extra-virgin olive oil

4 tbsp white wine

2 tbsp white wine vinegar

sea salt and freshly ground black pepper

potato

olives

tuna

Cook the potatoes, unpeeled, in simmering, salted water until tender. Whisk the olive oil, white wine, vinegar, salt and pepper together in a large bowl until slightly thickened. Drain the tuna, and flake it with a fork into bite-sized pieces.

Drain the potatoes and peel off the skin as soon as you can handle them – or don't bother peeling them at all – and cut into thick slices.

Toss the still-warm potatoes in the dressing. Using a pair of tongs, stack a few slices of potato on each plate. Top with a large spoonful of tuna so that it tumbles down the sides. Tuck in a few olives, and drizzle the lot with any remaining dressing.

Serves four

Japanese peppered tuna, served rare on cold noodles with the surprise of creamy avocado

main players:

2 x 250g (9oz) trimmed lengths

   sashimi-quality tuna

200g (7oz) dried soba noodles

1 avocado

staples:

1 tsp sea salt

1/2 tsp freshly ground black pepper

1 tsp Japanese sansho pepper

2 tbsp vegetable oil

2 tbsp mirin

2 tbsp soy sauce

1 tbsp rice wine vinegar or white wine vinegar

1 tsp sesame oil, plus extra to serve

Roll the tuna in the salt, pepper and sansho pepper. Heat the vegetable oil in a non-stick frying pan until quite hot and sear the tuna for 30 seconds on each side. Remove from the heat and let rest for 30 minutes.

Cook the soba noodles in a large pot of simmering water for 6–8 minutes or according to the instructions on the packet, until cooked but still firm, as for spaghetti. Drain well, rinse under cold running water and set aside.

Mix the mirin, soy sauce, vinegar and sesame oil in a large bowl, add the drained noodles and toss well.

Cut the avocado in half lengthwise and twist the two halves apart. Hit the stone with the blade of a large knife, then turn the knife to twist out the stone. Peel off the skin, cut the flesh into small cubes and toss lightly through the noodles.

Arrange the noodles in mounds on four small dinner plates. Slice the tuna finely, and arrange three or four slices on top. Drizzle with a little extra sesame oil and serve. **Serves four**

Sashimi-quality tuna is super-fresh and trimmed in neat blocks ready for cutting. It is available from food halls, superior fresh fish shops and Japanese food stores.

tuna

noodles

avocado

the slight bitterness of radicchio marries well with the saltiness of pancetta and the sweet-sourness of balsamic vinegar

radicchio

bread

prosciutto

main players:

3 heads radicchio

6 thick slices good country bread

6 slices pancetta or prosciutto

staples:

4 tbsp extra-virgin olive oil, plus extra for bread

2 tbsp balsamic vinegar or red wine vinegar

sea salt and freshly ground black pepper

Mix the olive oil, salt and pepper together to make a dressing.

Cut each radicchio in half lengthwise through the stem, then push down on the stems with the heel of your hand so they are slightly flattened out. Brush with the dressing. Place on or under a hot grill for 1–2 minutes, until they wilt, turning so that the outer leaves do not burn, but the inside still gets warm.

Brush the bread with a little extra olive oil and grill quickly on both sides. Remove from the grill and arrange on serving plates. Grill the pancetta for 15 seconds, until just warm. Layer the pancetta and radicchio on top of the grilled bread and drizzle the vinegar on top.

Serves six

trout

egg

potato

hard-boiled eggs play off the richness of smoked trout and potatoes

main players:

450g (1lb) smoked trout fillets

450g (1lb) potatoes

4 eggs

staples:

sea salt

4 tbsp extra-virgin olive oil

2 tbsp lemon juice

1 tsp Dijon mustard

1 tbsp tiny salted capers, rinsed

Use your fingers to flake the smoked trout into bite-sized pieces, carefully removing any skin and small bones.

Place the potatoes in a pot of cold water, add salt and bring to the boil. Simmer for 20 minutes or until tender. Remove from the heat and drain.

Meanwhile, place the eggs in a pot of simmering, salted water and cook for 8–9 minutes until hard-boiled. Remove and cool under cold running water. Peel and slice lengthwise, then set aside. Cut the potatoes into thick slices – peel them first if you like, but don't feel you have to.

Whisk the olive oil, lemon juice, mustard and capers in a bowl, and gently toss the potatoes in the dressing to coat.

Arrange stacked layers of potato and hard-boiled egg slices in the centre of each plate, top with the smoked trout and spoon on any remaining dressing.

Serves four

drained and hung yogurt turns into a fresh herb cheese overnight to serve with jewel-coloured peppers

main players:

1.2 litre (2 pints) Greek yogurt

3 mixed red and yellow peppers (capsicums)

8 sprigs fresh thyme

staples:

2 tbsp extra-virgin olive oil

1 tsp dried mint

20 small black olives

sea salt and freshly ground black pepper

grilled sourdough or warm Turkish bread

   to serve

Arrange a doubled piece of dampened cheesecloth or muslin over a bowl and tip the yogurt into it. Gather up the edges, tie with string and hang over the bowl for 6 hours or overnight, allowing the liquid to drip out.

Heat the oven to 200°C/400°F/Gas 6. Place the peppers on a baking tray and drizzle olive oil on top. Bake for 30 minutes until scorched and blistered. Place the peppers in a covered bowl for 10 minutes until cool enough to handle, then peel off the skins. Cut in half and discard the seeds. Cut the peppers lengthwise into wide strips.

Strip the thyme leaves from the stems. Untie the yogurt and mix with the thyme leaves, dried mint, salt and pepper.

Arrange the mixed peppers on each plate and top with a big spoonful of yogurt cheese. Scatter with small black olives. Serve with grilled sourdough bread or warmed Turkish bread. **Serves four**

yogurt

pepper

thyme

snappy green beans and earthy artichoke hearts in a nutty dressing with extra crunch

beans

artichokes

walnuts

main players:

250g (9oz) fresh green beans, trimmed

6 artichoke hearts, preserved in oil

175g (6oz) shelled walnuts

staples:

3 tbsp walnut oil or olive oil

1 tbsp red wine vinegar

sea salt and freshly ground black pepper

Cook the green beans in simmering, salted water, uncovered, for about 4 minutes, until tender. Drain and cool under cold running water.

Heat the grill and cook the artichoke hearts, flat side to the heat, until lightly scorched and warmed through.

Toast the walnuts in a dry frying pan until warm and fragrant.

Whisk the oil and vinegar with salt and pepper, and throw in the beans, tossing well to coat thoroughly.

To assemble, arrange half the green beans in the centre of a large serving plate, and top with a layer of artichoke hearts, grilled side up. Add a layer of remaining beans and scatter with the walnuts.

Serves four

red onion

beetroot

corn

warm roasted vegetables in a drizzle of capers and mustard – and you even get to eat the beetroot leaves

main players:

2 red onions

2 bunches medium beetroots with stems

2 corn cobs

staples:

4 tbsp extra-virgin olive oil

1 tbsp red wine vinegar or balsamic vinegar

1 tbsp tiny capers, rinsed

1 tsp Dijon mustard

sea salt and freshly ground black pepper

Heat the oven to 200°C/400°F/Gas 6. Peel the onions and cut in half, then cut each half into three wedges. Cut the green stems from the beetroots and wash the stems thoroughly to remove any grit. Scrub the beetroots but don't peel. Remove the husks from the corn and cut in half, crosswise.

Arrange the beetroots, corn and onion wedges in a roasting pan. Drizzle with a little of the olive oil, scatter them with salt and pepper and bake for about 1 hour, turning occasionally until tender and slightly caramelized.

Remove from the oven, and allow to cool for 10 minutes or so. Rub the skins off the beetroots and trim if necessary. Whisk the remaining olive oil with the vinegar, capers and mustard and add some salt and pepper to taste.

Cook the beetroot greens in a pot of simmering, salted water for 5 minutes until wilted. Drain well – really well – and divide between serving plates.

Arrange the corn, beetroots and onions on each plate. Spoon the dressing on top and serve still warm or at room temperature.

Serves four

Take the kitchen clock off the wall

and see what happens. Instead of sticking to the rigid hierarchies of lunch and dinner, you will immediately want to snack. This is a good thing. Snacks move easily from day to night; am to pm; breakfast to supper and back again. This is food you can dress up or down to suit. It's a return to primitive times, when humans were nomadic hunter-gatherers. Now, we forage in the refrigerator and the cupboard instead of the forests and fields. So let yourself go. Eat what you like, when you like. One of life's greatest pleasures is left-over chocolate mousse cake for breakfast, another is a fresh, juicy oyster at midnight. If you have no idea what the time is, just serve smoked salmon on toast. Besides, who says that eating three rich courses in a glamorous restaurant just before going to bed is good for you? Or that we thrive on greasy fried food within half an hour of waking up? Put that way, normal meals at normal mealtimes sound completely abnormal.

snacks

chicken

ginger

paper

yes, paper, to wrap up fragrantly scented, tender chicken wings

main players:

6 medium chicken wings

5cm (2in) piece of ginger, peeled

6 squares thick greaseproof paper, measuring
  30 x 20cm (12 x 8in)

staples:

3 tbsp soy sauce

3 tbsp Chinese rice wine or dry sherry

1/2 tsp salt

1/2 tsp sugar

1 tsp sesame oil, plus extra for parcels

peanut or vegetable oil for deep-frying

Cut the tips off the chicken wings, then cut each wing at the joint and trim into two neat pieces. Cut the ginger into cubes and push through a garlic crusher, to give 1 tablespoon of ginger juice.

Mix the ginger juice, soy sauce, rice wine, salt, sugar and sesame oil, and marinate the chicken pieces in the mixture for 3–4 hours, stirring every now and then.

Lay out one square of greaseproof paper (use two if the paper is very thin) at an angle so that a corner is facing you, and brush the centre lightly with sesame oil.

Place a well-drained chicken piece, skin-side down, in the centre and bring the left corner in to fold over the chicken, creating a straight left side. Fold in the top corner, creating a straight side, then the bottom corner. Roll over and tuck in the remaining right hand corner to seal the parcel.

Heat the peanut oil until very hot, and fry a few parcels at a time, for around 7 minutes, turning them as they cook.

Pile the chicken, still in its wrappers, on a platter, and serve as a snack, with finger bowls. Unwrap and eat. **Makes twelve**

a simple Spanish **tapas** snack of melting potatoes and **spicy** sausage, in **paprika-hot** juices

main players:

1 fresh chorizo sausage

450g (1lb) potatoes

1 onion

staples:

2 tbsp extra-virgin olive oil

1 garlic clove, peeled and squashed

sea salt and freshly ground black pepper

Cut the chorizo sausage into thick slices. Peel and finely chop the potatoes and onion.

Heat the olive oil in a frying pan and cook the chorizo, onion and garlic over a moderate heat for 10 minutes, stirring, until the onion is lightly golden.

Add the cubed potatoes and mix well. Add the salt, pepper and enough water to cover, then cook over a medium heat for 30 minutes until the water reduces to a thickened sauce and the potatoes are tender. Serve with crusty bread.

Serves four

chorizo

potato

onion

wok-fried, peppery squid, to serve with an icy-cold beer

main players:

450g (1lb) cleaned squid tubes

1 tsp ground Sichuan or black peppercorns

5 whole dried chillies

staples:

1 tsp sea salt, plus extra to serve

100g (3¹/₂oz) cornflour (cornstarch) or

plain flour

vegetable oil for deep-frying

Clean the squid tubes well and peel off any skin. Cut in half lengthwise, then cut into pieces measuring 2.5 x 5cm (1 x 2in) and use the tip of a sharp knife to score an even row of lines in the outer skin. This will make the squid curl up when fried.

Heat the wok and toast the peppercorns and 1 of the dried chillies until hot and fragrant. Place the peppercorns, chilli and salt in a mortar or a tough little bowl. Crush to a powder with a pestle or a wooden spoon and combine with the cornflour or plain flour.

Heat the vegetable oil until smoking. Toss the squid in the seasoned flour and shake off the excess. Fry the squid for about 1 minute (beware of spitting oil), then drain well on kitchen paper.

When the squid is cooked, deep-fry the remaining whole dried chillies until they turn crisp and dark (these are more for effect than for eating). Pile the squid high on a plate and top with the fried chillies. Scatter with a little extra sea salt.

Serves four

If you can find banana leaves, wipe them clean, cut into squares and roll into cones for serving, fastened with bamboo skewers.

squid

pepper

chilli

soft, fresh balls of cheese hit with **enough heat** to melt gently over **fragrant lemon** leaves, sparked up with a basil-green pesto

main players:

1 large bunch basil

8 large lemon leaves

2 balls mozzarella cheese, preferably

buffalo milk

staples:

2 tbsp pine nuts

2 tbsp grated Parmesan cheese

125ml (4¹/₂fl oz) extra virgin-olive oil,

plus extra for leaves

sea salt

Remove the basil leaves from their stems, and place in the food processor with the pine nuts and Parmesan. With the motor running, slowly add enough olive oil to make a fresh green paste. Add a little salt. The pesto can be stored in an airtight jar until required.

Heat a grill or cast-iron griddle. Wash and dry the lemon leaves, then brush both sides with a little olive oil. Slice the mozzarella finely and place one or two slices on each lemon leaf. Brush lightly with olive oil.

Grill, either on or under a hot grill, until the heat causes the cheese to softly melt. Remove from the grill, top each leaf with a teaspoonful of pesto and serve. You don't eat the leaf, okay? It's just there to give a smoky, lemony tang to the cheese.

Serves four

basil

lemon leaf

cheese

lettuce

scallops

prawns

crisp and crunchy prawns and mushrooms served in a lettuce cup to eat **in your hands**

main players:

1 head Iceberg lettuce

12 large raw scallops

12 medium raw prawns

staples:

10 dried Chinese shiitake mushrooms

2 tbsp peanut oil

4 tbsp chopped water chestnuts

3 tbsp oyster sauce

Soak the mushrooms in 250ml (9fl oz) of hot water for 30 minutes. Carefully separate 4 cup-shaped leaves from the lettuce, wash, dry, and chill until required.

Wash and dry the scallops, and trim off any dark bits. Devein the prawns by hooking out the black intestinal tract through the back of each with a fine bamboo skewer. Peel, then chop into rough cubes. Drain the mushrooms, reserving the water, discard the stems and slice the caps finely.

Heat the peanut oil in a wok until it starts to smoke. Add the prawns and scallops and cook for 15 seconds, tossing like mad. Add the water chestnuts and mushrooms and toss through.

Add the oyster sauce, stirring, and a little of the mushroom water if you need more sauce. Spoon the mixture into the chilled lettuce cups and serve immediately.

To eat, fold up the lettuce leaf and take a bite. **Makes four**

a simple mix of **marinated** olives brings the Mediterranean to the shores of your **cocktail glass**

olives

rosemary

garlic

main players:

450g (1lb) mixed olives in olive oil

8 sprigs rosemary or thyme

2 garlic cloves, peeled and squashed

staples:

3 tbsp extra-virgin olive oil

6 bay leaves

1 tsp dried oregano

When shopping for olives, make a nuisance of yourself. Get some big black ones, shrunken black ones, green Spanish queen ones, and any other type you can find.

Warm the olive oil in a frying pan with the rosemary sprigs, garlic, bay leaves and oregano and cook gently, stirring, for 5 minutes to infuse the oil.

Add the olives and toss well to coat in the spiced oil, then cook gently, stirring occasionally, for 5–10 minutes until soft and shiny. Use a slotted spoon to transfer olives, garlic, bay leaves and herbs to a rustic serving dish and serve hot, warm or at room temperature. **Serves four to six**

crisp wafers made of the noble Parmigiano Reggiano are used to sandwich succulent slices of prosciutto and ripe figs

parmesan

prosciutto

figs

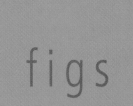

main players:

200g (7oz) Parmigiano Reggiano cheese,

  freshly grated

4 ripe figs

8 slices prosciutto

Heat the oven to 180°C/350°F/Gas 4. Lay an egg ring on a non-stick tray. Sprinkle an even layer of grated parmesan inside the ring. Remove the ring and use it to make a second wafer next to the first. Use these first two wafers as your guinea pigs, because you may have to adjust the heat of your oven to suit the rest.

Bake for 3–5 minutes, watching carefully, until the cheese has melted into a soft wafer shape. Remove from the oven while still bubbling, and leave for 1 minute. Carefully lift off the wafers and lay them on a wire rack to cool and harden. Adjust the oven temperature if necessary and continue the process until you have 8 wafers.

To serve, cut the figs into quarters. Lay 2 slices of prosciutto on top of a parmesan wafer on each plate. Top with 2 fig quarters and a final parmesan wafer, and serve. **Serves four.**

oyster

chilli

black bean

lightly steamed oysters in their shell with the **smoky**, **earthy taste** of black bean and a little red chilli

main players:

12 freshly opened oysters

1 tbsp Chinese black beans, rinsed

1 small red chilli, finely chopped

staples:

2 tbsp Chinese rice wine or dry sherry

1/2 tsp sesame oil

2 tbsp peanut oil

Arrange the oysters, still in their shells, on a heatproof plate that fits in your steamer. (Crumple foil beneath them and nestle them in it so they don't tip over.)

Mash the well-rinsed and drained black beans lightly with the chilli, rice wine and sesame oil. Divide the mixture equally between the oysters.

Bring the water in the steamer to a rolling boil and place the plate of oysters in the steamer. Cover and steam for 3–4 minutes, until the oysters plump up and start to give off their juices, but do not overcook.

Heat the peanut oil in a small pan until just smoking. Drizzle a little hot oil over each oyster. Serve 3 oysters per person.

Serves four

Chinese salted black beans are available by the packet in oriental food stores.

fresh little rolls with a **hint of chilli** will **save you** from being bored

main players:

8 medium prawns, raw or cooked

1 ripe avocado

1 packet rice paper wrappers

staples:

2 tbsp sweet chilli sauce

sea salt and freshly ground black pepper

Devein the raw prawns by passing a thin bamboo skewer through the spine and hooking out any thin black intestinal tract. If using raw prawns, poach them gently in a pot of simmering, salted water for 3–4 minutes until just cooked. Drain, cool and peel. If using cooked prawns, peel off the shells.

Cut the avocado in half lengthwise, remove the stone and peel. Cut the flesh into long strips.

Bring a pot of water to the boil and use tongs to dip eight stiff rice paper wrappers in and out of the water, one at a time. Lay them on a clean work surface, and top each with a prawn, a couple of strips of avocado, a little sweet chilli sauce to taste and a scattering of salt and pepper. Wrap up as if for a spring roll, tucking the ends in neatly as you go. Serve soon after making. **Serves four**

prawn

avocado

rice paper

It's late, and you haven't eaten for what seems like days. Don't stay out, go home. You can throw together a fast feast long before you can get a table at your favourite late-night haunt. If you can get a table.

Rice is good. Cheese is great. Toast is brilliant. Baconliness is close to godliness. The trick at supper is to eat exactly what you feel like eating. If that means three videos and take-away Chinese in bed, so be it. If it means a big bowl of pasta at the kitchen table, that's fine, too. If it means a glamorous post-opera supper and a seductive spread of dishes, well, go for it. Supper should either give you satisfaction at the end of the day, or the strength to prolong the evening into the night, should you want to do so. It's also very handy when you don't quite know what you want, but you know you want something. And you want it now.

supper

cod

parsley

tomato

fresh, fast, and cooked simply in the one pan

main players:

4 x 150g (5oz) firm white-fleshed fish

fillets, such as cod or hake

1 small bunch flat-leaf parsley

1 punnet red cherry tomatoes

staples:

2 tbsp extra-virgin olive oil, plus extra

for serving

2 anchovy fillets

2 tbsp small black olives

1 tbsp tiny salted capers, rinsed

Cut the fish fillets into nice chunky bite-sized pieces and set aside. Set aside a few leaves of parsley for garnish and finely chop the rest until you have 2 tablespoonfuls.

Heat the olive oil in a heavy-bottomed frying pan, add the anchovies and break them up with a wooden spoon. Add the fish and cook over a medium heat, moving the chunks around the pan as they cook.

Add the tomatoes, olives and capers and gently cook until the tomatoes soften and start to burst out of their skins.

Add the finely chopped parsley, then serve in shallow pasta bowls. Scatter with the reserved parsley leaves and drizzle with a little extra olive oil. **Serves four**

bitter chicory hits it off with rich and elegant

Gruyère and cream in a cheesy melting dish

chicory

gruyère

cream

main players:

8 heads of chicory (Belgian endives)

2 tbsp grated Gruyère cheese

3 tbsp double cream

staples:

1 tsp butter

sea salt and freshly ground black pepper

Heat the oven to 180°C/350°F/Gas 4. Trim the chicory ends neatly and cut in half lengthwise. Cook for 10 minutes in simmering, salted water until tender, then remove and drain off the excess water.

Lightly butter an ovenproof gratin dish, and lay the chicory in one layer, cut side down. Sprinkle with the cheese, salt and pepper, and spoon the cream on top.

Bake for 15–20 minutes until the cream is bubbling and lightly golden. **Serves four**

This works just as well with thin asparagus spears in season, topped with cream and grated Parmesan.

I call this **happy rice** – it's sunny, smily, mindlessly easy to make, and it takes me back to happy **holidays** in Spain

main players:

2 red peppers (capsicums)

150g (5oz) cooked ham

250g (9oz) Arborio rice

staples:

2 red onions

1 pinch saffron threads

1/2 tsp paprika

2 tbsp extra-virgin olive oil

500ml (18fl oz) hot chicken stock or water

sea salt and freshly ground black pepper

Heat the oven to 200°C/400°F/Gas 6. Roast the peppers for 30 minutes until scorched and blistered. Remove from the oven, cool slightly in a covered bowl and peel off the skins. Cut them in half, discard the seeds and cut the flesh into short strips.

Cut the ham into short strips. Peel and finely chop the red onions. Pound the saffron and paprika with a spoonful of hot water until dissolved.

Heat the oil in a lidded frying pan and cook the onion over a moderate heat for 10 minutes, stirring, until soft. Add the raw, unwashed rice and toss to coat. Add the hot stock or water and the spice liquid, and bring to the boil.

Add the red peppers, chopped ham and salt and pepper and stir well. Reduce the heat to low, cover and simmer for 20 minutes, stirring occasionally, until the rice is cooked and the liquid has been absorbed. Serve in bowls with a fork and spoon. **Serves four**

red pepper

ham

rice

a quick Italian frittata of frizzled bacon and lots of Parmesan tossed through pasta and pan-fried until golden

main players:

350g (12oz) macaroni, penne or rigatoni

4 thin rashers bacon

3 tbsp grated Parmesan cheese, plus extra to

serve

staples:

6 eggs

sea salt and freshly ground black pepper

macaroni

bacon

parmesan

Cook the pasta in boiling, salted water, according to the packet instructions, until tender but firm to the bite. Drain well, then rinse in cold water and drain well again.

Cut the bacon into short strips, and fry in a non-stick frying pan until crisp. Remove the bacon with a slotted spoon, leaving the bacon fat in the pan.

Break the eggs into a bowl and beat lightly. Add the cheese and stir. Add the drained pasta to the bowl and toss well. Add the bacon, salt and pepper and toss again.

Tip the egg and pasta mixture into the pan in which you cooked the bacon and cover. Cook over a gentle heat for 15 minutes.

Check that the bottom is lightly golden and the top is set. If the top is still runny, hold the pan under the grill for 1 minute. Sprinkle the frittata with the extra Parmesan and serve hot, in big wedges.

Serves four

a great trick – throw in handfuls of fresh green leaves at the last minute to wilt into juicy greens that cut the strength of the blue cheese

linguine

rocket   gorgonzola

main players:

150g (5oz) gorgonzola or Roquefort-style cheese

2 bunches rocket

450g (1lb) dried linguine or spaghettini

staples:

125ml (4 1/2 fl oz) milk

1 tbsp butter

freshly ground black pepper

Trim off the stems of the rocket, and wash and dry the leaves.

Mash or chop the cheese and set 1 tablespoonful of it aside. Combine the remaining cheese in a pan with the milk, butter and pepper. Stir with a wooden spoon until the sauce melts together. Add a few spoonfuls of the pasta cooking water, stir through, and keep warm.

Cook the linguine in plenty of boiling, salted water, according to the packet instructions, until tender but still firm to the bite. When the pasta is cooked, throw the rocket leaves into the pasta pan for a few seconds until they wilt, then drain both the pasta and rocket together. Divide between four pasta bowls.

Spoon the hot sauce on top, toss lightly, and sprinkle on the reserved cheese.
Serves four

beans

pork

garlic

green beans wok-tossed with a little spicy pork and a slow chilli burn

main players:

450g (1lb) green beans or long snake beans

200g (7oz) minced pork

2 garlic cloves, peeled and squashed

staples:

1 tbsp soy sauce

1/2 tsp cornflour (cornstarch)

1 tsp sugar

3 tbsp vegetable oil

1 tbsp Chinese rice wine

1/2 tsp chilli oil or less, to taste

sea salt and freshly ground black pepper

Trim the tips off the beans and cut into 15cm (6in) lengths. Cook in simmering, salted water for 2 minutes, then drain and cool under cold running water.

Mix the pork with the soy sauce, cornflour, sugar, salt and pepper.

The trick to this dish is to have both the wok and the oil hot at all times, and to cook quickly, tossing constantly. Heat one-third of the vegetable oil in a wok. When it is hot, stir-fry the beans quickly with a pinch of salt for 1 minute over a high heat, until wrinkled.

Remove the beans and reheat the wok, adding the remaining vegetable oil and the garlic cloves. When hot, discard the garlic and add the pork mixture, stir-frying quickly for 3 minutes until it darkens.

Add the rice wine and chilli oil and stir through. Return the beans to the sauce and stir-fry briefly until mixed. Serve with plenty of steamed rice. **Serves four**

prawns

tofu

steamed blocks of tofu topped with fresh prawns – a light, healthy meal put together in minutes

onions

main players:

12 small raw prawns

8 small blocks fresh tofu

2 spring (green) onions, finely chopped

staples:

4 tbsp soy sauce

1 tbsp sesame oil

1 tbsp oyster sauce

1 tbsp sweet chilli sauce

1 tbsp crisp-fried shallots (optional)

Devein the prawns by inserting a fine bamboo skewer through the back and hooking out any black intestinal tract. Peel them, leaving the tails on.

Drain the tofu and stack one block on top of another until you have four double-storey blocks. Arrange them on a flat heatproof plate that will fit into your steamer. Place the prawns on top or in a separate steamer.

Steam over bubbling water for 5 minutes, until the tofu is heated through and the prawns are just cooked, turning from transparent to opaque.

In the meantime, combine the soy sauce, sesame oil, oyster sauce and chilli sauce in a small pan and heat, stirring, without allowing to boil.

To serve, use a fish slice to carefully place a block of tofu on each plate. Arrange the prawns on top. Spoon the hot sauce on top and scatter with spring onions and fried shallots, if using. **Serves four**

beans

prosciutto

polenta

tender broad beans spooned generously over foothills of golden polenta

main players:

1kg (2lb 4oz) broad beans, shelled

4 slices prosciutto

350g (12oz) instant polenta

staples:

2 tbsp extra-virgin olive oil

2 onions, finely chopped

250ml (9fl oz) chicken stock

1 tbsp butter

sea salt and freshly ground black pepper

freshly grated Parmesan cheese to serve

Heat the oil in a heavy-bottomed frying pan, add the onions and cook until they soften. Add the broad beans, sea salt, pepper and chicken stock. Cover and cook gently for 15 minutes, until the broad beans are tender and there are barely any juices. Cut the prosciutto into strips, add to the broad beans and cook for 1 minute.

To make the polenta, bring 1.8 litres (3 pints) water seasoned with ½ teaspoon salt to the boil. Stirring constantly, pour in the instant polenta in a slow, steady stream, like sand. Reduce the heat to very low, and stir with a wooden spoon for 6–8 minutes, until the polenta pulls away from the sides of the pan. Stir in the butter, then taste. Add pepper, and more salt to taste.

Spoon huge dollops of polenta on each warmed serving plate, and then top with the broad bean and prosciutto mixture. Sprinkle with grated Parmesan and serve.
Serves four

a simple fried egg and a sprinkling of herbs

turns spaghetti into supper

main players:

400g (14oz) spaghetti or tagliatelle

4 eggs

1 handful sage leaves

staples:

2 tbsp olive oil, plus extra for pasta

1 tbsp butter

Parmesan cheese for shaving and grating

sea salt and freshly ground pepper

Cook the pasta in plenty of boiling, salted water, according to the packet instructions, until firm but tender to the bite. Towards the end of the cooking time, heat half of the olive oil and the butter in a non-stick frying pan. Crack the eggs carefully into the pan, cover and cook gently until the whites have set, and the yolks are cooked but still runny.

Using a vegetable peeler, shave off 8–12 shavings of cheese and set aside. Grate 2 tablespoons of cheese and set aside.

Drain the pasta well and divide between four pasta bowls. Toss with a little extra olive oil, the grated cheese and salt and pepper, and top each one with a fried egg (you may have to cut any joined ones apart). Top with the Parmesan shavings.

Heat the remaining olive oil and very quickly sizzle the sage leaves in it until crisp. Pour the oil and sage leaves over the pasta, and serve immediately. Serve the remaining wedge of Parmesan at the table with a small hand grater. **Serves four**

spaghetti   eggs   sage

a jolly big poached sausage, sliced over juicy, spicy, herby lentils

main players:

300g (10oz) brown or green lentils, soaked
  for 30 minutes

1 large smoked sausage, such as Saucisse
  Lyonnaise, or 4 smaller ones

1 bunch flat-leaf parsley, finely chopped

staples:

2 tbsp extra-virgin olive oil

1 onion, finely chopped

400g (14oz) can plum (roma) tomatoes

1/2 tsp ground coriander

1/2 tsp ground cumin

sea salt and freshly ground black pepper

Heat the olive oil in a pan, add the onion and cook for 15 minutes over a moderate heat until soft. Add the tomatoes and their juices, drained lentils, coriander, cumin, salt, pepper and 500ml (18fl oz) cold water, and bring to the boil, stirring. Reduce the heat to low and cook for 20 minutes.

Prick the sausage and poach in simmering water for 30 minutes to heat through.

Stir most of the chopped parsley into the lentils, and divide them between four plates. Drain the sausage, peel off and discard the skin and slice into thick rounds. Arrange the slices on the lentils and serve with the remaining parsley on top. **Serves four**

sausage

parsley

lentils

There are things that lie patiently around the house – like onions and eggs – until you need them. Or things you buy every few days – like bread and lemons – that can actually feed you in many ways. Or things that you can't live without – like tomatoes and olive oil – that can bring your cooking to life. Treat this chapter as if it's that lovely, kind, but missing person in your life who is always on call to answer all those boring questions you're too embarassed to ask anyone else, like how to peel a tomato, make a Caesar salad dressing or poach the perfect egg.

wine

bread

eggs

olive oil

onions

lemons

tomatoes

standards

wine

It's time we took to the bottle and treated wine as a great ingredient, using its layers of flavours to brighten our cooking in any number of ways, not least by the glass, direct to the cook. Add a good splash of white or red wine at the start, and allow it to bubble and reduce to one quarter its volume. This way, the alcohol evaporates, and you are left with lots of flavour to add to casseroles, soups and sauces.

As a flavour zapper: Use red and white wine for stews, poaching and marinades, but don't stop there. Use *shao hsing* (Chinese rice wine) for marinating chicken and for Chinese cooking and sake (Japanese rice wine) for Japanese marinades and sauces.

As a salad dressing: Start with a good vinegar (wine, champagne, sherry) in a bowl. Add a pinch of sea salt and a grind of black pepper. Whisk in a splash of dry white wine or champagne and a few chopped herbs, then drizzle in extra-virgin olive oil or a good nut oil, whisking constantly.

As a poaching liquid: Poach fish, prawns and crabs in a broth of one part white wine to four parts water, along with diced carrot, celery and parsley.

As a sauce: Deglaze a cooking pan by splashing some wine into the hot pan and scraping up the crusty sediments left after browning chicken or lamb. Bring it to the boil, stirring, then strain. Whisk in a little butter for richness and serve.

As a meal: Bread, cheese and wine. Bliss. Try crusty sourdough with Manchego cheese and a red Rioja; dark rye with goat's cheese and Gewurztraminer; or toasted sweet brioche with Gorgonzola and Sauternes.

Spiced pears

Combine 250g (8oz) sugar, 600ml (18fl oz) red wine, 450ml (16fl oz) water, 2 cinnamon sticks, and a few cloves and peppercorns, and bring to the boil, stirring. Boil for 1 minute, then remove from the heat. Peel 6 pears lengthwise, leaving the stem, cut out the base core, and place snugly in the liquid. Simmer gently for 30 minutes or until the pears are tender, then leave to cool in the syrup. Serve with fresh cream, ricotta cheese or coffee ice-cream, or slice and serve with duck and lamb.

Summer/winter marinade

Combine 120ml (4fl oz) white wine, 3 tbsp olive oil, 1 crushed garlic clove, 1 tbsp chopped parsley, sea salt and pepper to marinate fish, chicken, lamb and beef for summer grilling. Change to red wine in winter to give flavour to lean meats like chicken before some long, slow cooking.

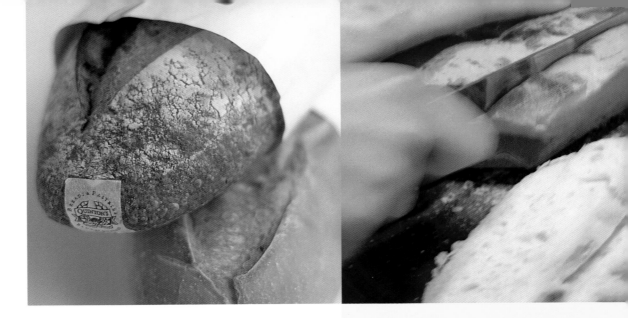

bread

Great bread has a life longer than the day you buy it. It can live again and again, drowned in soups; dunked in hot, milky coffee; baked with eggs and milk; torn into pieces and tossed with olive oil, tomatoes and olives. So start with good bread: tough sourdough, rich brioche, strong Italian casalinga bread, ciabatta, pide, focaccia and fragile French ficelle.

As a snack: Grill thick door-stopper slices of slightly stale Italian casalinga bread and top with herb-strewn mushrooms, chicken livers or baked beans.

As a sauce: Heat milk, butter, cloves, herbs and a chopped onion to boiling point, then leave until cool. Strain and whisk in fresh white breadcrumbs until thick but still liquid. Serve with roast chicken.

As a salad: Cut thick fingers of country-style bread and fry with finely chopped bacon until crisp. Toss into a salad of torn green leaves with a dressing of mustard, red wine vinegar, garlic and olive oil.

As a soup: Cover thick slices of sourdough bread with thin slices of Gruyère cheese and grill until melting. Place in soup bowls and pour a good chicken soup on top. Scatter with parsley.

As a crumb: Turn stale bread into chunky crumbs that beat hands down the sawdust sold by that name in supermarkets. Cut off the crusts and cut the bread into chunks. Leave on a baking tray in a very low oven until completely dry, without browning. Cool and whizz briefly in a food processor, or crush by hand and store in an airtight jar until you're ready for them.

French toast

Dip 4 long slices of baguette, cut on the diagonal, into a batter of 2 eggs, 120ml (4fl oz) milk and a little ground cinnamon. Fry quickly in a little butter on both sides until crisp and golden. Serve with a drizzle of honey, a dusting of icing sugar, fresh sliced fruits or a handful of berries.

Italian bread salad

Grill 2 thick slices of country-style bread and cut into cubes. Peel 3 ripe tomatoes and chop roughly. Combine with 1 finely chopped red pepper, 1 tbsp rinsed capers, 1 crushed garlic clove, 2 anchovy fillets, 1 tbsp black olives, 2 tbsp red wine vinegar and 3 tbsp extra-virgin olive oil. Toss the bread in the salad and serve at room temperature.

top anything with a perfectly poached egg

eggs

Eggs are the pale and beautiful symbols of purity, rebirth and instant gratification. One crack, and you have breakfast. Another crack, and a sauce is bound, a soufflé rises, a cake is baked and fresh pasta lies hanging from the broom handle. Use free-range eggs, because I don't care what they say, I know the hens are happier.

As a stew: Break a few eggs on top of a baked Mediterranean vegetable stew (aubergines, courgettes, tomatoes) and return to the oven until almost set.

As a soup: Heat a good chicken stock to a high simmer. Beat 2 eggs and slowly pour them into the broth, whisking constantly, letting them cook into long thin strands. Scatter with parsley and serve with garlicky grilled bread.

As a sandwich: Mash a few hard-boiled eggs with sea salt, pepper and very good mayonnaise while still warm, then spread on fresh white or rye bread.

As a garnish: Make a really thin omelette in a wok or frying pan with 3 eggs flavoured with a little soy sauce. Roll it up, cut into thin strips, and use as a garnish for noodles, soups and stir-fries.

As a snack: Hard-boil two dozen quail eggs and serve peeled with a little spiced salt (try cumin or paprika) for dipping and chilled champagne for sipping.

As a hangover cure: Combine 1 fresh, raw egg yolk, a splash of brandy, a shake of Tabasco, a squeeze of lemon juice and a grind of pepper and down it in one gulp. This is the only good reason to give up drinking that I have yet come across.

The perfect poached egg

Fill a broad, shallow pan with water and bring to the boil. Add 2 tbsp white vinegar and turn off the heat. Break open 4 eggs and slip them quickly into the water one at a time. Cover and leave for 3 minutes. Remove the eggs from the water with a slotted spoon and drain on kitchen paper. Trim off any rought edges with scissors, and serve.

The perfect omelette

Lightly beat 3 eggs, sea salt and pepper together with a fork. Add 1 tsp butter to a good pan. When it foams, add the eggs and stir lightly with a fork over a constant high heat. Use the fork to lift the edges as they set and tilt the pan to allow the runny egg to spill down into the gap. Add any fillings at the last minute, then slide onto a warm plate and jerk the pan so that one side folds over as you tip it. Serve immediately.

olive oil

Olive oil is the new butter, but there is room for both in our kitchens and on our tables. If we spent as much on one bottle of extra-virgin olive oil from Italy, Spain or Greece as we spent on a decent bottle of wine, we'd have a joy for a month or two instead of for an hour or two. Better still, we'd remember using it.

As a mash: The next time you mash spuds, use extra-virgin olive oil (at room temperature, don't heat it first) instead of butter. Gorgeous.

As a relish: Keep your best olive oil on the table and drizzle lightly over fresh vegetable and bean soups, pasta, and roasted vegetables.

As a pasta sauce: Chop 6 ripe tomatoes and combine in a pan with 115ml (4fl oz) extra-virgin olive oil, lots of fresh basil, a little garlic, sea salt and black pepper, and cook, stirring gently, for 15 minutes. Toss with your favourite pasta.

As a marinade: Combine garlic, chopped parsley and coriander, lemon juice, ground cumin, paprika, sea salt and pepper with extra-virgin olive oil and use to marinate fish, prawns, lobster, lamb chops and chicken wings before grilling.

As a salad dressing: Whisk extra-virgin olive oil with white wine or sherry vinegar, sea salt and pepper and a little Dijon mustard.

As a vegetable dressing: Whisk extra-virgin olive oil and red wine vinegar with sea salt, pepper, rinsed capers, fresh thyme, oregano and pine nuts.

Spaghetti with olive oil, garlic and chilli

Cook 400g (14oz) spaghetti in boiling, salted water until firm but tender to the bite. Heat 4 tbsp extra-virgin olive oil in a heavy pan, add 4 squashed garlic cloves and 1 chopped red chilli, and warm through. Drain spaghetti, pour oil mixture on top, add some chopped parsley and serve.

Fresh herb mayonnaise

Whizz 2 egg yolks and 1 tbsp lemon juice in a food processor, and add up to 375ml (13fl oz) olive oil very slowly, drop by drop, as you whizz, until half the oil has been incorporated. Now you can add it a little faster in a slow, steady stream, still whizzing until you have a thick, creamy paste. Add sea salt and pepper to taste, and add more lemon juice to taste. Finely chop fresh basil, thyme or chives and fold through the mayonnaise. Serve with eggs, cold meats, vegetables and fish.

onions can save your life

onions

If you get home hungry, just put a frying pan on the stove. Throw in a little olive oil, a couple of squashed garlic cloves and a finely chopped onion or two. Get all that sizzling, then work out what you can turn it into.

As a stew: Add chicken pieces, white wine, chicken stock and beans and cook until tender.

As a pasta sauce: Add a few roughly chopped and skinned pork sausages and a can of tomatoes, cook until thick and dump onto bowls of pasta.

As a supper: Add some chopped fresh tomatoes and herbs and cook until stewy, then serve as a sauce poured over grilled slices of aubergine, courgette and red peppers.

Sweet onion confit

Slice 4 big white onions finely and cook in 25g (1oz) butter and 450ml (16fl oz) dry white wine in a heavy-bottomed pan over a low heat for 30 minutes, covered, until the onion is soft and melting. Add sea salt and pepper to taste. To use as a relish, cook , uncovered until the liquid has evaporated. To use as a creamy sauce, add 120ml (4fl oz) hot chicken stock or water and cook for another 5 minutes.

As a risotto: Add Arborio rice and toss to coat. Add some peas, then slowly add chicken stock and cook slowly for 30–40 minutes. Serve with plenty of freshly grated Parmesan cheese.

As a soup: Add finely chopped leeks, carrots, potatoes and celery, cover with boiling water and cook until soupy.

Onion and black olive frittata

Slice 3 big white onions finely and cook in 25g (1oz) butter for 30 minutes over a low heat until soft and melting, then cool. Arrange in a thick layer in a lightly oiled quiche tin and scatter with 2 tbsp stoned black olives. Beat 4 eggs with 250ml (9fl oz) cream and 250ml (9fl oz) milk. Add salt, pepper and ground nutmeg and pour on top. Bake for 45 minutes until puffy and golden. Serve warm.

As a savoury mince: Add minced veal, chopped bacon, white wine, tomatoes, nutmeg, a little flour and cook for 1 hour, stirring, then serve as a sauce to polenta, pasta, rice or grilled bread.

get bitterand twisted with a lemon

lemons

Lemons are the reason why our mouths water. Use them to zap up grilled vegetables, make cocktails and spike up sauces and dressings. Get bitter and twisted and give your taste buds a big dipper ride. There's no point being sweet if you can't be sour as well.

As a dressing: Whisk 4 tbsp lemon juice with 5 tbsp extra-virgin olive oil, sea salt, freshly ground black pepper and 1 tbsp finely chopped parsley and drizzle over shellfish, vegetables or mixed green leaves.

As a marinade: Combine 120ml (4fl oz) white wine, 2 tbsp lemon juice, 2 tbsp olive oil, 1 crushed garlic clove, 1 tbsp chopped parsley, sea salt and pepper and use to marinate fish, chicken, lamb and beef for summer grilling.

As a margarita: Shake 3 tbsp lemon (or lime) juice with 3 tbsp tequila and 2 tbsp Cointreau over crushed ice, and serve in a salt rimmed glass. Makes one.

As an appetiser: This is weird, but cute. Slice 2 lemons and chill the slices well. Arrange on a tray and top each slice with 1 teaspoon of salmon caviar. Top with a little sprig of dill and serve with shot glasses of frozen sake or vodka. You just suck the caviar off the lemon and discard the lemon.

As an accompaniment: When grilling or pan-frying shellfish or fish, grill or pan-fry a few slices or halves of lemon as well, to serve at the same time.

As a cleaning agent: Rub half a cut lemon over your chopping board to eat up the odours of onion, garlic and fish.

Lemon butter sauce

Combine 2 tbsp lemon juice with 3 tbsp chicken or vegetable stock in a small saucepan, and heat, stirring. When hot, whisk in 150g (5oz) cold butter, a few small pieces at a time, without allowing the sauce to boil. Taste for lemon juice, salt and pepper, and serve over asparagus or salmon.

Caesar salad dressing

Place 1 egg in simmering water for 1 minute, then remove, crack into a bowl, and whisk with 2 tbsp lemon juice, sea salt, pepper, and 100 ml (3½fl oz) extra virgin olive oil until smooth. Add 1 tbsp grated parmigiano and 2 finely chopped anchovies, and drizzle over crisp cos leaves.

bite into a fresh
ripe red
tomato

tomatoes

Go berserk with them when they're in season, and go to the canned ones when they're not. If you have a spare hour, roast a few in the oven to intensify their flavour, for sauces, pasta or to go with a grill or a roast. Or just bite into a fresh, ripe red tomato as if it were an apple.

As a salad: Slice a large red or yellow tomato into four slices, then reassemble, layering fresh basil leaves and fresh mozzarella cheese between each slice. Dress with extra-virgin olive oil, sea salt, pepper and balsamic vinegar.

As a roast: Cut a heap of plum (roma) tomatoes in half, drizzle with extra-virgin olive oil and roast in a low oven for 1 hour. Serve with fresh ricotta cheese and pesto.

Oven-dried tomatoes

Cut 1kg (2lb 4oz) plum (roma) tomatoes in three lengthwise slices, salt them very lightly and bake in a single layer in a very low oven (80°C/180°F/Gas½) for 10 hours or overnight until semi – but not fully – dried. Store in an airtight jar, covered in olive oil (remember to press down firmly to remove any air) and eat within the week, with crusty bread and cheese, in salads, pasta, or on toast.

As peeled: Cut lightly around the circumference with the tip of a sharp knife and dunk in a pot of simmering water for 10 seconds. Remove, and peel off the skin.

As a fine dice: Peel the tomatoes and cut in half. Squeeze out the seeds and juice, and cut the flesh into small dice.

Tomato jam

Cut 1kg (2lb 4oz) tomatoes in half, squeeze out most of the seeds, then roughly chop the flesh. Place in a saucepan with 2 tbsp brown sugar, 2 tbsp mustard seeds, 2 tbsp red wine vinegar and 3 tbsp olive oil and bring to the boil. Lower the heat and simmer, bubbling, for up to 1 hour, stirring occasionally, until thick and jammy. Add salt and pepper, cool, and store in airtight jars in the fridge. Use within a week.

As a fry: Cut big oxheart tomatoes into thick slices and fry briskly in a non-stick pan with a touch of olive oil until scorched. Stack with fried eggs, fresh thyme and crisp bacon.

As a sauce: Toss cherry tomatoes into a frying pan. Add olive oil and garlic and cook until they soften. Use for lamb and pasta.

general index

ready reference